The Excel Data and Statistics Cookbook

Third Edition

Larry A. Pace

TwoPaces.com

Anderson SC

Pace, Larry A.

The Excel Data and Statistics Cookbook, Third Edition

ISBN 978-0-9886300-0-0

Published in the United States of America by

TwoPaces.com
102 San Mateo Dr.
Anderson SC 29625

Preface and Acknowledgments

I decided to write this book as soon as I began using Excel 2010, and immediately after finishing and publishing my last two books on using Excel for statistics (Pace, 2008; Pace, 2010a). But life and other writing projects intervened. Through some job changes and a resulting reduced teaching load in the summer of 2012, I finally carved out the time needed to finish what I had started a few years earlier. On returning to this project and digging deeper into the statistical functionality of Excel 2010, I was pleasantly surprised. During the time I was writing and revising this book, Microsoft introduced Excel 2011 for Mac and released a preview version of Excel 2013 for Windows. Wanting to be as current as possible, I downloaded the preview version of Excel 2013 and used that version for the screen captures shown in this book.

Microsoft made Excel a more capable and accurate statistical package with Excel 2010, 2011, and 2013. The statistical functions were expanded and most were brought up to industry standard. I am aware (and frequently reminded by some of my colleagues who disdain spreadsheets) that Excel is not a fully-featured statistics package. For my own research, I typically use a combination of SPSS and the statistical programming language R. I have written books illustrating the use of both of these for basic statistics (Pace, 2012a; Pace, 2012b). However, even though I do my own statistical analyses using other technologies, I use Excel on an almost daily basis. For data manipulation, data exploration, and data cleaning, Excel is preferable to other alternatives. I also find Excel to be a very good tool for teaching basic statistics, even when the student will eventually use some other statistics tool for data analysis.

I confess to being a bit of a spreadsheet addict, having used Excel since it came out more than 20 years ago. Before that, I used Quattro Pro, Lotus 1-2-3, PC Calc, and even SuperCalc for the CP/M operating system (I know I am dating myself). I was personally disappointed that Excel did not provide better statistical functionality as the program was revised over the years. Although there is still some room for improvement, Excel 2010 and newer versions are far superior to the previous versions, especially regarding the statistical functions and features.

This book shows screens from the Excel 2013 preview version running in the Windows 7 environment. As of this writing, Windows 8 has just been released, and should make quite a stir with its focus on touch screens. According to Microsoft, Excel 2013 is optimized for this new operating environment. I will let you know what I think as soon as I have upgraded and begin work on the inevitable fourth edition of this book!

For the sake of continuity, I also illustrate the use of the "legacy" functions that still work in Excel 2013 as well as previous versions from 97 to 2011. My approach is very much hands-on. Although I do not cover statistical theory in detail, I do show the relevant formulas and explain how they are translated into Excel functions and formulas.

Creating interactive plug-and-play templates for various statistical analyses is a hobby of mine, and I have posted a variety of these, along with the larger data sets for this book, on my web site:

http://twopaces.com

In order to keep things as simple as possible, I use no macros or third-party add-ins in this book or in my statistics templates, though I do occasionally show the output produced by the statistical add-in MegaStat, which is distributed by McGraw-Hill. MegaStat was written by Professor J. B. (Deane) Orris of Butler University, and in my opinion is the best statistics add-on for Excel. At a price of only $10, MegaStat turns Excel into a full-featured statistics package. Appendix D of this book shows you how to acquire and use MegaStat. Many students have difficulty choosing the correct statistical test, so I have added a new appendix (Appendix E) with a flow chart to help with that choice.

I find many Excel spreadsheet models on the Internet use a bit of sleight of hand, for example, hiding cells from the user or making it impossible to see the formulas and functions by protecting cells and worksheets. My approach is completely different: I hide nothing. Even though I often protect the cells containing the formulas to keep users from accidentally changing or erasing the cell, I make all cell contents visible. I intend my templates as transparent teaching tools (Pace, 2010b). If you want to, you can see everything in each template I make. I want users to explore them, because by studying the template, users can learn how Excel works and how to calculate and interpret statistical tests, as well as build their own templates when necessary.

No book is ever the work of a single individual, even when there is a single author. I am grateful for the external reviews of Alex Russell (University of Sydney), Dr. Kathleen Andrews (University of the Rockies), Dr. Lê Xuân Hy (Seattle University), Dr. Luke Rosielle (Gannon University), Dr. Rick Jerz (St. Ambrose University), Dr. James E. Hoffman (University of Delaware), Dr. Karl Kelley (North Central College), and Dr. Boris Djokic (Keiser University). I would like to acknowledge the support of my program chair at Keiser University, Dr. Susan Adragna, and my dean, Dr. Sara Malmstrom.

To my wife Shirley Pace, I express my devotion and love. Shirley likes reading Stephen King novels, while I prefer reading and writing about statistics and research. We often sit on the sofa with our respective reading choices. I once told a student about this and she replied, "Well, Dr. Pace, they're the same really—both scary!"

I welcome e-mail from my readers, and love hearing from both students and instructors. Please let me know what you think of this book, and let me know if you find any grammatical, typographical, or factual errors. My e-mail address is larry@twopaces.com.

About the Author

Dr. Larry Pace is a statistics author, educator, and consultant. He is a Graduate Professor at Keiser University, where he teaches doctoral classes in statistics, quantitative methods, and mixed-methods research. He has more than 100 publications including books, articles, chapters, and reviews. He has also written hundreds of online tutorials and reviews.

He has received multiple awards for teaching, service, and research, including the Servant Leadership Award from Anderson University, the Psi Chi Professor of the Quarter award from Louisiana Tech University, and a medal and certificate from the European Quality Management Foundation. He was named a National Quality Professional by Rochester Institute of Technology, and he received the Oral Presentation Award from the Society of Automotive Engineers.

Dr. Pace earned the Ph.D. from the University of Georgia in psychological measurement (applied statistics) with a content major in industrial-organizational psychology. In addition to his statistics background and teaching, Dr. Pace has been credentialed to teach a wide variety of classes including psychology, management, leadership, sociology, and mathematics. Over the past 35 years, Dr. Pace has taught at Keiser University, Argosy University, Walden University, Ashford University, University of the Rockies, Clemson University, Tri-County Technical College, Austin Peay State University, Capella University, Louisiana Tech University, LSU–Shreveport, the University of Tennessee, Rochester Institute of Technology, Monroe Community College, Cornell University, Rensselaer Polytechnic Institute, and the University of Georgia. He was an instructional development consultant for Furman University in 2007. In 1997, Dr. Pace was invited by the Finnish government to lecture at the University of Jväskylä and to serve as a dissertation examiner for Dr. Taina Savolainen, whose dissertation he had earlier supervised at LSU-Shreveport.

In addition to his academic career, Dr. Pace worked for Xerox Corporation from 1979 to 1988. Serving as a personnel psychologist, organization effectiveness consultant, and organization effectiveness manager, he won the Xerox Special Merit award for his contributions to the employee involvement, total quality management, and product delivery processes. He also worked for a private consulting firm from 1999 to 2002, serving as an organizational development consultant, researcher, trainer, and facilitator. Dr. Pace has also been an external consultant to International Paper, Xerox Canada, Compaq Computers, Tandem Computers, AT&T, Lucent Technologies, Allied Signal, UOP, Southwestern Electric Power Company, ARKLA Gas Company, the U.S. Navy, Christus Schumpert Medical Center, Libbey Glass, the Louisiana Department of Education, the Tennessee Valley Authority, and other organizations.

His current research interests include human error in data entry, the use of technology in statistics education, and an investigation of students' and faculty members' attitudes toward plagiarism and other forms of academic dishonesty.

Dr. Pace is married to Shirley Pace. The Paces share their home with six cats and a dog. The Paces are community volunteers with Meals on Wheels. When he is not busy doing statistics, writing about statistics, or helping others with their statistical analyses, Dr. Pace enjoys building statistical models in Excel, figuring things out on the computer, learning new statistical techniques, playing mathematical puzzles and word games, playing music (guitar, banjo, flute, recorder, mountain dulcimer, and harmonica), tending his vegetable garden and giving away his produce, reading (mostly nonfiction because truth is always stranger than fiction), writing poems, hosting gatherings of friends and family, and cooking on the grill.

In a dimly remembered past, before there were personal computers and cell phones, Dr. Pace carried a slide rule and programmed a mainframe computer using punch cards and FORTRAN-IV. He was also a long haired member of a famously local rock band from high school until his sophomore year in college. He finally realized he was better at statistics than music, so he decided to go to graduate school in order to become a professor and a professional statistician and to remain an amateur musician.

Selected Books by Larry Pace

- *The Excel Data and Statistics Cookbook* (3rd. edition) (TwoPaces.com, 2012)
- *Beginning R: An Introduction to Statistical Programming* (Apress, 2012)
- *Point-and-Click! A Guide to SPSS for Windows* (5th edition) (TwoPaces.com, 2012)
- *Using Microsoft Word to Write Research Papers in APA Style* (TwoPaces.com, 2012)
- *Doing Basic Statistics with R* (Lulu.com, 2011)
- *Statistical Analysis Using Excel 2007* (Pearson Prentice Hall, 2010).
- *The Excel 2007 Data and Statistics Cookbook* (2nd edition) (TwoPaces.com, 2008).
- *Introductory Statistics: A Cognitive Learning Approach* (TwoPaces.com, 2007).
- *Basic Statistics for the Behavioral and Social Sciences* (2nd edition) (TwoPaces.com, 2005).
- *Using Excel for Basic Statistics: A Visual Guide* (2nd edition) (TwoPaces.com, 2005).
- *The Excel Statistics Cookbook* (TwoPaces.com, 2004).
- *The Investment Approach to Employee Assistance Programs* (with Stanley J. Smits) (Quorum Books, 1992).

Brief Contents

Table of Contents

1 A Statistician's View of Excel

In this chapter, you learn everything you need to get started using Excel for data management and basic statistics. If you want to find out more about Excel or want to obtain a free trial version of Excel, visit the Excel home page here:

http://office.microsoft.com/en-us/excel/

At the outset, a caveat is in order: Excel is not a dedicated statistics package. Instead, it is a general-purpose spreadsheet program. With the release of Excel 2010, Microsoft responded to many complaints, enhanced the statistical functionality of the program, and corrected many of the statistical shortcomings of previous versions. Excel's *unified problem space* is ideal for teaching and learning basic data management and basic descriptive and inferential statistics. Dedicated statistics packages, programs, and languages are often expensive and usually demand a significant learning curve. That said, if you are doing professional-level data analysis, you need a professional statistics package like SPSS, SAS, or Minitab, or a statistical computing language like S-Plus or R. On the other hand, most computers today come with a spreadsheet program, and spreadsheets are straightforward. For day-to-day data analysis and basic statistics, Excel is unsurpassed. The flexibility of the spreadsheet makes it useful for many applications that may be unavailable or very expensive with a standard statistical package, and spreadsheets allow you to integrate statistical analyses with other business models.

Those who are not familiar with spreadsheets might think of this: A spreadsheet serves a purpose for quantitative information similar to the function that a word processor serves for words. With a spreadsheet, you can organize, store, update, analyze, present, and evaluate quantitative information. The electronic spreadsheet, not the word processing program, was the first breakthrough business application for the personal computer. Even if you have never used a spreadsheet program, you will find Excel relatively easy to learn. Be warned that learning a spreadsheet program is somewhat harder than learning a word processing program like Microsoft Word or a presentation program like Microsoft PowerPoint. By contrast, a spreadsheet is easier to learn than a dedicated statistics package such as SPSS or a relational database program like Microsoft Access.

About This Book

This book is not intended to teach you basic statistics—though you will probably learn or relearn something about statistics by reading this book and working through the examples and exercises. Moreover, this book is not intended to teach you everything there is to know about a spreadsheet program, though you will learn quite a bit about Excel by the time you are finished. Instead, this book is intended for students, teachers, and researchers who want to learn how to use the data management features and statistical functions and features of Excel. Interactive worksheet templates, workbooks containing the Excel files for most of the examples and many of the exercises in this book, and many other statistics resources can be found at the companion web page located at the following URL:

http://twopaces.com/cookbook.html

There are many excellent web-based Excel tutorials, and you should look there first if you are completely new to spreadsheet programs. Links to several free web-based Excel tutorials can be found at the companion web page. It is a good idea to bookmark the companion page and the statistics help page so that you will have easy access to the data files for this book and to the worksheet templates and other statistics resources:

`http://twopaces.com/stats_help.html`

As with any other computer program, the best way to learn Excel is to use it. When you are stuck, remember that **F1** is the universal Windows help key, and it launches Excel Help. For the technically-minded, Excel provides ample opportunities for intermediate, advanced, and even expert applications through the use of Visual Basic, user-defined functions, and macros. To keep things simple and transparent, this book and the associated worksheet templates make no use of macros or third-party add-ins.

If you have used a dedicated statistics program like SPSS or Minitab, you will recognize the data views of SPSS and Minitab as spreadsheets. If you have used SPSS, you know there are separate files and windows for the output, the data, and the syntax. However, you might be interested to learn that the Excel interface combines the data view, the variable view, and the output viewer into what I call a *unified application space*, in which a user can see the data, the formulas, and the output without changing windows. In addition to its low cost and wide availability, Excel's unified application space makes it incredibly useful for learning and teaching basic statistics. The student can see the data, the formulas, and the results all in the same place at the same time, and can instantly see what happens to the results when the data are modified. Also, the statistics you learn in Excel can easily be combined with other business models, such as those you might find in operations management, strategic planning, financial analysis, decision theory, or quality control.

Conventions Used in This Book

This book makes use of a shortcut way to refer to using Excel's menu-driven ribbon structure. For example, you may need instructions to find the **AutoSum** tool in the **Editing** group of the **Home** ribbon. A more direct way to summarize these steps is **Home > Editing > AutoSum**. "The Bottom Line" text boxes are used throughout this book to summarize key points. To make them easy to locate, these boxes have solid borders, gray shading, and are in Calibri font. These quick summaries will be helpful for readers interested in "cutting to the chase" by reading a bulleted outline, and for those looking for a quick refresher for a given procedure,. When you must type into an Excel cell or the Formula bar, I show this in `Courier New font`. Courier New font is also used to set off the names of Excel functions, such as `AVERAGE(Range)` as well as to display web addresses. **Boldface** type is used to indicate a menu item or group label that the user clicks on or locates in the Excel interface. When you need to press a key or a combination of keys on the keyboard, **boldface** is combined with angle brackets, such as **<Enter>** or **<Ctrl> + T**. An exception is the use of function keys such as **F1** or **F4**, which will be shown in **boldface** without brackets. **Boldface** type is also used to refer to the titles of the tabs such as **Home**, **Insert**, and **Data**, as well as to the names of the associated groups such as the **Workbook Views**, **Show/Hide**, **Zoom**, **Window**, and **Macros** groups on the **View** ribbon.

The Evolution of the Excel User Interface

Over the years, as the features of Excel grew, the interface became more and more cluttered with toolbars, icons, and menus. With the 2007 version of Office, Microsoft introduced a new file format and a completely redesigned user interface (see Figure 1-1). Users of previous versions will find all of the functionality they are used to in Excel 2010 (Figure 1-2) and the newer versions for Mac (Excel 2011) and PC (Excel 2013). The features are occasionally in new and sometimes unexpected places. This book refers primarily to the Excel 2013 workbook interface shown in Figure 1-3. If you are still using Excel 2003 or an even earlier version, you might find the interfaces of Excel 2007 and newer versions surprising, perhaps even a little shocking, initially. A good way to become familiar with Excel is to open a blank workbook file and follow along with the examples in this book. Excel 2013, which was in preview when I wrote this, is very similar to Excel 2010 in appearance and functionality (see Figure 1-3).

Figure 1-1. The Excel 2007 interface

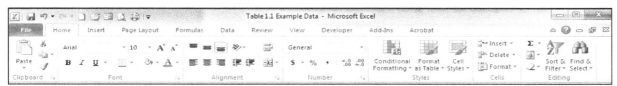

Figure 1-2. The Excel 2010 interface

With Excel 2010, Microsoft replaced the Office Button from Excel 2007 with the **File** tab (see Figure 1-2). The **File** tab remains in Excel 2013 (see Figure 1-3). The Excel 2013 interface is very similar to that of Excel 2010, so the transition should not be difficult for most users. Note the major features of the Excel interface, and make sure you can locate the ribbon, the tabs, the groups, the Formula Bar, the Name Box, the worksheet tabs, and the Status Bar. Clicking the **File** tab opens what Microsoft calls the "backstage view" of your workbook file (see Figure 1-4). This is where you print, save, close, and open workbook files. This is also where your most recently used Excel workbooks will appear, and where you can gain access to Excel Options.

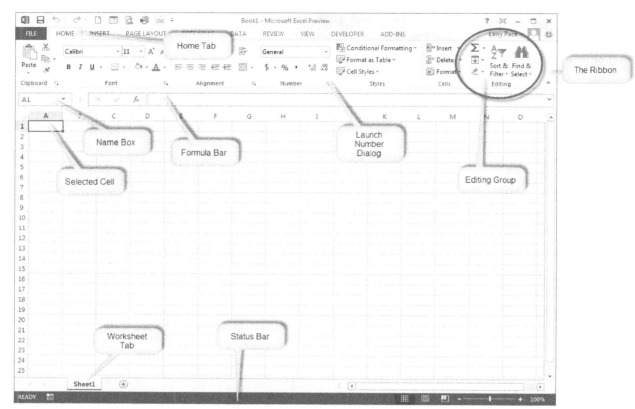

Figure 1-3. The Excel 2013 interface

Figure 1-4. The "backstage view" of Excel 2013

As mentioned previously, Microsoft introduced the "ribbon" with Office 2007. The ribbon remains in Excel 2010 and Excel 2013 (see Figure 1-3), and replaces the "Standard Toolbar" from earlier versions. The ribbon provides a super menu that uses a tab-and-group hierarchy. On the ribbon, tabs organize groups, and groups organize related functions, tools, commands, and options. The groups are displayed in separate boxes on the ribbon. To illustrate, clicking on the **Home** tab reveals the **Home** ribbon with **Clipboard**, **Font**, **Alignment**, **Number**, **Styles**, **Cells**, and **Editing** groups. Holding the cursor over a particular icon in a specific group brings up a box with a description of the command, for instance the box describing the Format Painter shown in Figure 1-5.

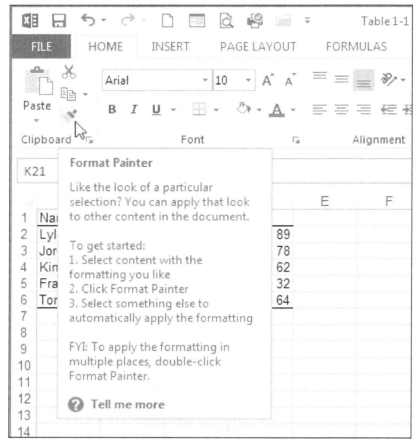

Figure 1-5. Pausing the cursor over the Format Painter icon pops up a description

Many of these boxes are illustrated, and some of them display keyboard shortcuts for accessing the given command. If a particular command is currently unavailable, it will be "grayed out." To see an example of this, click on the **Review** tab in a new workbook and see that the options in the **Comments** group for deleting and selecting comments are not active because there are no comments in the worksheet (see Figure 1-6).

Figure 1-6. Unavailable options are "grayed out"

The icons and labels in the available groups expand or contract to make optimum use of the screen real estate for various screen resolutions. With smaller screen sizes, the labels and icons will be reduced in size and detail, and you will need to click dropdown arrows to access the available options. In the bottom right corner of many of the groups is a little "Launch Dialog" button represented as a square with a diagonal arrow (see the labeled icon in the **Number** group in Figure 1-3, page 16). When you click such buttons, you will launch a dialog or a task pane with additional features or customization options. Holding the cursor over the button will reveal an illustrated description of these features.

When you add elements such as tables, charts, or pictures to your worksheet, a specific **Tools** menu will appear in the title bar above the associated ribbon tab, and a new tab or tabs like **Format** for pictures and **Design** for tables will be added to the ribbon. After you have added a picture, chart, or table, the associated tab and ribbons will always be available, though not always visible. To see them again when they are not visible, simply select the object. In Chapter 2, you will examine in detail some of the very useful things you can do with tables. Charts and graphs and the pivot table tool are discussed in Chapter 3, and you will learn there that the **Chart Tools** also provide customization options through additional groups.

The brief introduction to the Excel 2013 interface you get from this chapter is enough to get you started with data management and basic statistics, and applies to other uses of Excel and other Office programs as well. Even if you find the new interface a little strange at first, you will learn to appreciate its consistency, especially across the suite of Microsoft Office applications.

Unlike the old Standard Toolbar, the ribbon is not completely customizable, but this is not necessarily such a bad thing. New tabs and groups will be added to the ribbon only when you install add-ins or elements such as tables or charts. You cannot resize or move the ribbon, though you can minimize it. However, you also cannot accidentally delete or "lose" the ribbon the way you could the Standard Toolbar.

If you prefer a larger working area on the screen, you can minimize the ribbon by double-clicking on any of the ribbon tabs (except the **File** tab) such as **Home**, **Insert**, or **Page Layout**. After you minimize the ribbon, only the tabs will appear. When you click on a tab, the ribbon will reappear, "floating" atop the worksheet. The ribbon will vanish when you return to the work area. If you decide that you want the ribbon to be maximized again, double-click on one of the tabs. In Excel 2013, this functionality has been moved to

---

THE BOTTOM LINE

- The File Tab provides access to printing, opening, and saving workbook files.
- The File Tab also provides access to Excel Options.
- The ribbon replaces the Standard Toolbar of previous versions.
- The ribbon provides a tab-and-group hierarchy to all the menus available in Excel.
- Icons and labels in the available groups on the ribbon will shrink or expand as the screen resolution changes.
- Many groups have an additional Launch Dialog button at the bottom right corner.
- All options are available even when the screen size is reduced, but the user may need to click on a dropdown arrow to see the options.
- The ribbon can be minimized by double-clicking on any ribbon tab. Double-clicking on any tab restores the ribbon.
- When a command is not currently available, it will be "grayed out."

The Anatomy of a Worksheet

In the following sections, you will find what goes into a worksheet, how to navigate the workbook interface, the various ways you can format cells and their contents, and how to work with cells and cell ranges. You will also learn how to use a shortcut called a *named range*. Last, you will learn the differences between relative and absolute references, and how to use these differences to your advantage.

Newer versions of Excel can hold a vast amount of information. Earlier versions were limited to 256 columns and 65,536 rows per worksheet, but Excel 2010 and more recent versions can include a whopping 16,384 columns and 1,048,576 rows per worksheet. That is about 1,000 times more cells than the earlier versions. Microsoft somewhat understatedly called this the "Big Grid." An Excel workbook file can have multiple "plies" or separate worksheets. One navigates through these worksheets by clicking on the worksheet tabs at the bottom of the workbook interface (see Figure 1-1). As if 16,000 columns and 1 million rows were not enough, by default you can have up to 255 worksheets in a single workbook file. You can have even more than that if you have enough system resources. Indeed, Excel now handles a large amount of information.

If you find the worksheet tab labels "Sheet1, Sheet2, and Sheet3" unhelpful, you can double-click on a tab and rename it to something more useful. You can also right-click on the tab to rename the worksheet, as well as provide a color-coding scheme, much like physical notebook binder tabs. You can rearrange the sheets by clicking on a tab and dragging it to a new position. You can add more worksheets when you need them by clicking on the last tab, as shown in Figure 1-7.

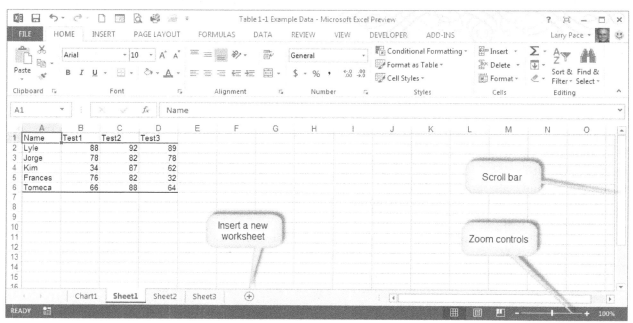

Figure 1-7. Navigating the workbook

The actual work area of a spreadsheet beneath the Name Box and the Formula Bar consists of ***rows*** and ***columns*** located beneath the column letters and to the right of the row numbers. The intersection of a row and a column is a ***cell***. The columns of the worksheet are labeled with letters from left to right, beginning with A – Z, then AA – AZ, then BA – BZ, and so on, all the way up to XFD in Excel 2010. The rows are numbered from top to bottom beginning with 1. To find the address or "reference" of a particular cell, refer to the column letter(s) first and the row number second in locating, navigating to, or naming a cell or a range of cells. By examining Figure 1-7, you can quickly determine that cell A1 is the upper left cell of the worksheet work area. The reference A1 appears in the Name Box. The dark borders and the highlighted row and column labels show that A1 is the active cell.

A cell in a worksheet can contain any of the following kinds of information:
1. A number (such as 12, 3.14, or the current date–Excel stores dates as numbers).

2. Text (such as "Question_1," "Date," or "Name,"–obviously without the quotes).
3. A formula (such as = 1 + 1 or = B1 + B2).
4. A built-in function (such as AVERAGE, STDEV, or FREQUENCY).
5. A pointer to other cells and ranges in the same worksheet or another worksheet (such as =A132 or =Sheet2!$B$2). These pointers display in the current cell the contents of the cell to which one is pointing. You can even refer to cells or ranges in a different workbook file by enclosing the workbook name in square brackets ([ ]) before the individual sheet name. Here is an example:

```
=[Workbook_Name.xlsx]Sheet1!$A$2
```

As you gain experience with Excel, you will ultimately learn that you can "concatenate" information within a given cell, and combine more than one type of data in a single cell, but a cardinal rule for statistical applications is that a single cell should contain a single value, whether typed directly into the cell, or calculated as the result of some function or formula.

Enter numbers and text by selecting the cell and then typing directly into the cell. You can also select the cell and click in the Formula Bar to enter or format numbers or text. Excel recognizes numerical entries and right-justifies them by default. Excel also recognizes text and left-justifies it by default. If you want Excel to recognize a number as a text entry, you can precede the number with a single quote ('). Excel will helpfully give you an error warning (a little green triangle in the upper left corner of the cell) to let you know that you have stored a number as text, which is precisely what you want to do on occasion, such as using 2011, 2012, and 2013 as column headings for three consecutive years.

If you are entering numbers, remember that a single cell should have a single number in it. Text entries in cells should be limited to small amounts of text, used as labels for the values in adjacent cells or column headings. You can also type more than one line of text in a given cell (see Figure 1-8) by using a feature called text wrapping. Select a cell or a range of cells and then click **Home** > **Alignment** > **Launch Alignment Tab**. Check the box in front of "Wrap text." The formatting will attempt to fit everything it can on each line, and will start another line when no more words will fit on the line. When you need to start a new line as in an address (See Figure 1-4), press <**Alt** > + <**Enter**> to start a new line in the same cell.

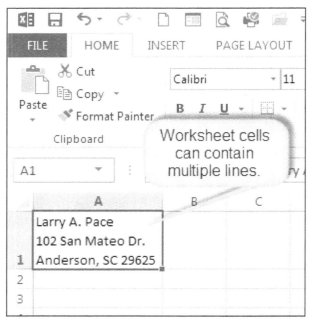

Figure 1-8. A worksheet cell may contain multiple lines

If you need to insert even longer text entries, you should consider using a text box (**Insert > Text > Text Box**) that will float on top of your worksheet.

You can format cells and their contents by changing the font size and font face, the color, the cell background and border formatting, the alignment, number formatting, and other characteristics. Excel provides predefined cell styles accessible from the **Styles** group. Click **Home > Styles** (see Figure 1-9). Additional styles include conditional formatting and table formatting options.

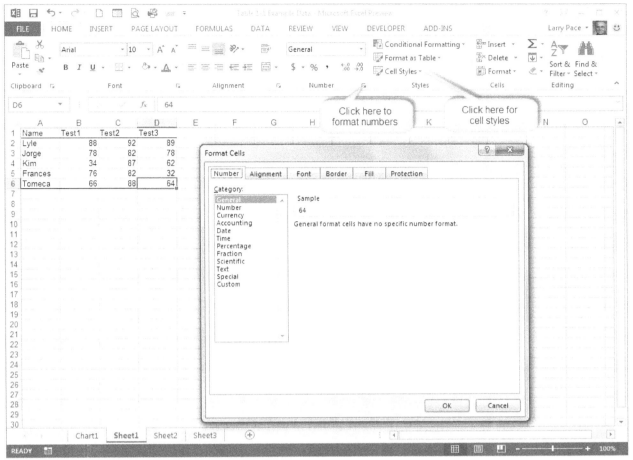

Figure 1-9. Formatting numbers and accessing various cell styles

It is possible to merge and unmerge cells (**Home > Alignment > Merge & Center**). You can also center text across a selection of cells without merging cells by selecting **Home > Alignment** and then clicking on the **Launch Alignment Dialog** icon at the bottom right of the **Alignment** group. In the resulting **Format Cells** dialog box on the **Alignment** ribbon, select **Horizontal**, **Center Across Selection**, and then click **OK**.

To format a cell, you can right click on a cell or selected range to launch a context-sensitive menu (Figure 1-10) and then select **Format Cells**. Remember that you can also get to cell formatting options by clicking on the "Launch Dialog" boxes at the bottom right of the **Font**, **Alignment**, and **Number** groups in the **Home** ribbon.

To enter a formula, a function, or a cell or worksheet pointer, you signal to Excel that you are not entering text or a number by preceding the entry with an equals sign (=). When you enter formulas, functions, or cell pointers, the formula, function, or pointer will appear in the Formula Bar and the result (Value View) will appear in the cell.

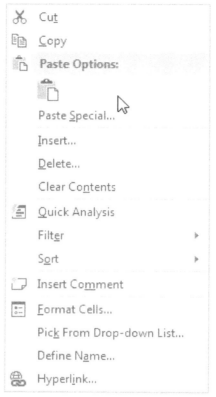

Figure 1-10. Context-sensitive cell menu

In addition to putting "stuff" into specific worksheet cells, you can also add elements that are not attached to any specific cell. These include charts and graphs, pictures, clip art or other graphics, text boxes, drawings, word art, equations, and other objects. These objects "float" on top of your workbook file and can be moved, sized, copied, and deleted.

Cell contents can be copied, deleted, and moved. You can move a cell's contents to another location by cutting and then pasting, or you can select the cell, move the cursor to the highlighted cell border (note that the cursor becomes a four-way arrow) and then simply click and drag the cell and drop it in its new location. You can use the Format Painter (**Home > Clipboard > Format Painter**) to copy the formatting from one cell to another cell or cells. Keyboard shortcut commands, such as **<Ctrl> + C** for copy, **<Ctrl> + X** for cut, and **<Ctrl> + V** for paste, also work in Excel. You can find the associated command icons for these operations in the **Clipboard** group of the **Insert** ribbon.

Although you can simply type stuff into cells in a haphazard fashion, you will ultimately find it most helpful to organize the information. Related information can be placed in columns and rows in such a way that you can apply formulas, functions, and tools most efficiently.

THE BOTTOM LINE
- The intersection of a *row* and a *column* is called a *cell*.
- Cells are referenced by the column letter(s) first and the row number second, as in cell D32.
- Each cell should contain one entry only. Cells can contain numbers (dates are also stored as numbers), text, functions, formulas, and pointers to other cells or other worksheets.
- Numbers are right aligned by default.
- Text is left aligned by default.

- Formulas and functions appear in the Formula Bar when the cell is selected.
- Cells and cell contents can be formatted in many ways.
- Cell contents can be copied, moved, and deleted.
- Cells can be merged and unmerged, and text can be centered across a selection of cells without having to merge the cells.
- Other elements not attached to specific cells can also be added to the worksheet. These elements include text boxes, graphics, equations, and other objects. These elements can also be copied, moved, and deleted.

Doing Math in Excel

Doing math in Excel requires the use of specific conventions. Excel provides the following basic mathematical operations. You simply type the arguments and operators into the cell where you want the result to be displayed. These operators can be freely mixed with each other and with functions and formulas. Remember that you need to start with an equals sign to get the calculations to work. Arguments can be actual values, cell references, or names:

- *Addition* (indicated by the + sign), as in = 2 + 3 or =B1 + B2 or =Price + Tax.
- *Subtraction* (indicated by the − sign), as in = 6 − 4 or =C22 − C23.
- *Division* (indicated by the / sign), as in = 66 / 2 or = D19 / A12 or =MSB / MSW.
- *Multiplication* (indicated by the * sign), as in = 2 * 2 or = B1 * B7.
- *Exponentiation* (indicated by the ^ sign), as in = 2 ^ 8 or = A21 ^ A22.

Excel also provides an operator for *negation* (such as the negative sign in front of −4.3) and one for *percent*. The minus sign − is used both for negation, as in the value −2, and for subtraction as in 6 − 4. The % operation will result in the division of the cell entry by 100, and the result displayed followed by the % symbol. In Excel, mathematical operations and functions are evaluated from left to right in a cell. The standard order of mathematical operations in Excel is parentheses, exponentiation, multiplication, division, addition, and subtraction (PEMDAS–recall the mnemonic *Please Excuse My Dear Aunt Sally*). You can force the operations into any desired order by the use of parentheses. You will want to examine the many other mathematical, financial, and logical functions available in Excel, but in this book you will stay with the basics described above and the additional statistical functions and tools introduced throughout the book.

Remember, you signal to Excel that the cell or Formula Bar entry is NOT text or a number by *starting* with the equals sign, =. Mathematical operations are performed by entering values or cell references (either cell addresses or range names) as the "arguments." As indicated above, to add 2 and 2 in Excel, you select an empty cell where you want the result to appear, type = 2 + 2, and then press **<Enter>** or **<Tab>**, or simply select another cell. To subtract the value in cell B2 from the value in cell B3, you select an empty cell, then type = B3 − B2 and press **<Enter>**. To find the square of the value in the cell you have named X, you type in = X ^ 2 in an empty cell and press **<Enter>**.

Excel also has other operators that you can mix with the native operators discussed above. Some of the most useful for statisticians are:

- *Summation*, performed by the SUM function, as in =SUM(Test1) or =SUM(A1:A11).
- *Mean*, found by the AVERAGE function, as in =AVERAGE(Test1) or =AVERAGE(A1:A24).

- *Square root*, calculated by the SQRT(Value) function, as in = SQRT(Sheet2!B132) or =SQRT(81).
- *Sum of squares*, performed by the DEVSQ function, such as =DEVSQ(Test1).

In the examples above, you can place in the parentheses the actual data values separated by commas, cell references separated by commas or colons (for consecutive ranges), or a range name. "Value" in the square root function is replaced by a number, a cell reference, or the name of a cell or formula. Built-in functions are updated dynamically so that if any value in the data set is changed, all formulas or functions referring to that value will re-evaluate and instantly display the new result.

Working with Ranges and Names

It is possible to work with more than one cell at a time. A series of consecutive cells is a ***range***. One kind of range is a set of consecutive values in a single column or a single row. This one-dimensional list of values is an ***array***. To refer to an array, you use a colon to separate the references of the first cell in the array and the last cell of the array. Examine the data in Figure 1-11 and notice that the label and data values for Test1 are in Column B, starting in Row 1 and ending in Row 6.

	A	B	C	D
1	Name	Test1	Test2	Test3
2	Lyle	88	92	89
3	Jorge	78	82	78
4	Kim	34	87	62
5	Frances	76	82	32
6	Tomeca	66	88	64
7				

Figure 1-11. Test 1 scores and the column label are in the range B1:B6

We refer to this array with the reference B1:B6. It does not hurt to include the column label in the range with the values, because Excel will ignore the label when calculating statistics, and will use it when reporting them if you ask for a label.

When you find yourself referring to the same range repeatedly, and when you want to clarify what is being used in formulas and functions, you can use a shortcut called a ***named range***. After you have named a range, you can refer to the name in functions and formulas. The values for Test1 could be given the name "Test1" (without the quotes, obviously). A very easy way to name a range is to select the range with your mouse, to click in the Name Box (Figure 1-11), and then to type the desired name directly in the Name Box. Press <**Enter**> to apply the name to the selected cell or range. It is okay to reuse the column label for the name of the range, so you can type in "Test1" (without the quotes). We can similarly name the ranges for the students' names, Test2, and Test 3. After naming a range, you can include them in functions and formulas by typing in the name rather than the cell references. You can click the dropdown arrow to the right of the Name Box to see all the named ranges and objects and to select any of them. Figure 1-12 shows the list of named ranges as described above.

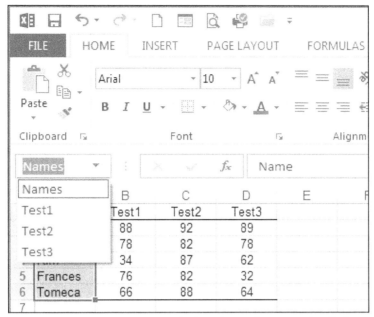

Figure 1-12. Clicking on the arrow at the right end of the Name Box reveals all the named objects in the workbook. Clicking on the name selects the object

Named ranges have another advantage. If you decide to change a selected range, for example by adding or deleting records, you only need confirm that the named range includes the data for the new information and edit the name to include the new information if it does not. After that, any formulas or functions that refer to this range will still work properly, and will include the updated information.

Ranges can also include two or more columns and two or more rows. A tabular range with two or more columns or rows is called a *table*. You refer to a table by referring to the first (upper left) and last (lower right) cells. For example, return to Figure 1-10 and look at all the data. You could refer to the range A1:D6 and select the entire data table. It is also possible to name a table. You might want to call this range "Scores." Later in this book, you will learn about using a special kind of named Excel object also simply called a table, but providing additional features besides those of a named range.

When you create a table or chart or add a picture, it is named automatically, and the object can be selected via the Name Box and the Name Manager. If you find that you need to modify or delete a name, you can click on the **Formulas** tab and access the Name Manager (**Formulas > Defined Names > Name Manager**). You can also use the Name Manager to create names, although the shortcut of typing the desired name for cells and ranges directly into the Name Box is simpler. For those interested in more advanced applications of names, note that in addition to naming ranges of cells, note that you can give names to single cells, to constants, and even to formulas. It is possible to use the OFFSET function to create a *dynamic range*, a device used in some of the statistics templates for this book, but not illustrated here. You will not see named formulas in the Name Box, but you can see and edit them via the Name Manager. This book only discusses naming individual cells and cell ranges. Excel also automatically names certain objects added to the workbook, as discussed below.

In addition to their many other advantages, named ranges make it possible to write formulas that others can understand when they are using spreadsheets you create. This is very helpful for the computation of statistics and building Excel formulas more similar to the equations in statistics books. Range names can contain letters, numbers, and underscores, and must start with a letter. The names cannot contain spaces or special characters.

Here is a warning about naming a range. You should not attempt to name a range something that will conflict with Excel's own conventions for naming cells. For example, you might think quite logically that Q1 would be a good name for Question 1 in a survey, and that Q2 would be a good name for Question 2. The problem is that Q1 and Q2 are already reserved by Excel as labels for specific cells in the worksheet. You will confuse Excel (and yourself) if you try to name a range with a cell reference, so that is something to avoid. If you type a cell reference such as Q1 in the Name Box, Excel will simply move the active cell to Q1. This is a great way to move around in your workbook, but not a good way to name ranges. Because Excel now provides more than 16,000 columns, and makes use of letters for column labels, up to column XFD. This means that many range names that work in early versions of Excel, such as "day1," "day2," and "day3," will conflict with cell references for actual worksheet cells using the references DAY1, DAY2, and DAY3. One way to avoid this with three letter names followed by a number is to use the names "day_1," "day_2," and "day_3." You may simply prefer to use at least four letters in your range names and prevent this confusion altogether.

Other than the restriction that the names cannot conflict with normal cell references and that they must contain only letters, numbers, and underscores, there are no additional restrictions to named ranges. You can even call a named range "Sheet2," "Frequency," or any other Excel function or structural name, but caution dictates against doing so.

THE BOTTOM LINE
- You can create and store a name for a cell, a range of cells, a constant, or a formula.
- The easiest way to name a cell or a range is to select it and then click in the Name Box, type the desired name, and press **<Enter>**.
- Selecting the name in the Name Box selects the particular named cell, range, or object.
- Names can be used in place of cell references in formulas and functions.
- Excel names tables and charts as special named objects in the workbook file. These names also appear in the Name Box
- It is possible to create dynamic ranges using the OFFSET function (this is not discussed further in this text).
- Names can be also be defined, edited, and deleted by selecting **Formulas > Defined Names > Name Manager.**

Relative and Absolute References

A cell or range reference can be *relative* or *absolute*. The default reference in Excel, such as the reference to cell A1, is a relative reference. Sometimes, you want to use relative references; other times you want to use absolute references. On many occasions, you want to use both absolute and relative references at the same time, as illustrated below. When you name a range, as we discussed in the previous section, the named range will always use absolute references.

Relative references allow you to take advantage of the dynamic updating and indexing features of Excel. When you copy a formula, function, or cell pointer from cell A1 to a different cell, any relative cell references in A1 will be indexed or incremented by Excel to refer to their new location in the worksheet. This is a great feature because you very often want to copy a formula from one cell to another or to a range and have the formula instantly update to refer to the new cell locations. Sometimes, however, that is exactly what you do *not* want to happen, because you want the reference a particular cell or range to be *absolute*.

To illustrate both relative and absolute references, let us say you refer to a cell, perhaps cell A12, which contains the mean of an array of numbers (see Figure 1-13).

Figure 1-13. Average of the 11 values is in cell A12

You want to write a formula to calculate a deviation score for each score in the column by subtracting the mean from the value in the adjacent cell. If you write a formula in cell B1 to calculate the deviation score for the first value by typing in = A1-A12, the formula will work perfectly. However, that formula cannot be pasted to cell B2 and still work properly, because the indexing will change the formula to = A2-A13. Because cell A13 is empty, the deviation score will not be correct (Figure 1-14).

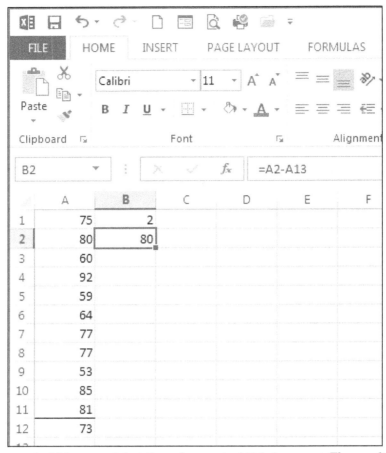

Figure 1-14. The reference to A2 is correct, but the reference to A13 is incorrect. The resulting deviation score is 80 – 0 = 80, instead of 80 – 73 = 7

To avoid this problem, you can change the reference to cell A12 from relative to absolute by going back to cell B1 and changing the formula to = A1-$A$12. The dollar signs indicate an absolute reference to column A and row 12. Now, when you copy the formula from cell B1 to cell B2, the formula will change to = A2-$A$12, indexing the first reference and keeping the second reference constant. You can simply type in the required $ signs to change either the row or column references (or both) from relative to absolute.

The corrected formula from cell B2 appears in the Formula Bar (see Figure 1-15). The deviation score is now also correct. Pasting this formula to cells B3:B11 results in the correct calculation of all the deviation scores. The way this works is that pasting the formula into cell B3 will cause the correct formula =A3-$A$12 to appear in the Formula Bar (and the Formula View), and the correct deviation score, 80 – 73 = 7 to appear in the cell.

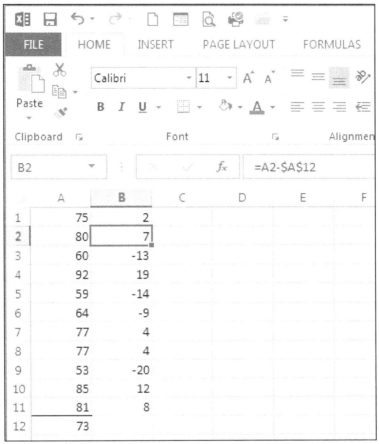

Figure 1-15. Correct formula combines relative and absolute references. The deviation scores are now calculated correctly

You can use a convenient keyboard shortcut to change an address from relative to absolute and back again. Select a cell with a formula in it that uses a relative reference, say cell B1 as discussed above. Then click in the Formula Bar, select the cell reference you want to make absolute (which is cell A12). Press the **F4** key. Note that Excel adds the $ signs, changing the entry to $A$12. Pressing **F4** again changes the entry to A$12, changing it to a relative column reference combined with an absolute row reference. Pressing **F4** once more changes the reference to $A12, with an absolute column and relative row reference, and pressing **F4** one last time changes both references back to relative ones. Thus, the **F4** key acts like a toggle with four states. The more you use Excel, the more you will appreciate the flexibility of relative and absolute references. Note that when you use named ranges, those ranges will always make use of absolute references.

As mentioned previously, when you need to point to a cell or range in a different worksheet in the same workbook, you use an absolute or relative reference that includes the worksheet title followed by an exclamation point (!), such as

```
=Sheet2!A32 or =Sheet3!$B$7
```

We also discussed that it is possible in a function or formula to refer to a cell or range in a different workbook file. When that is necessary, the pointer should use square brackets to surround the name of the file, as illustrated below:

```
=[Book2]Sheet3!$A$1:$A99
```

If you use a reference like the one above, when you press <**Enter**>, you will be prompted for the location of the other workbook file, and will have to navigate to it for each such reference. In other words, when you refer to another workbook, unless both workbooks are open at the same time, the pointer will not work automatically as do the ones within the same workbook. It is possible to automate the updating of Excel workbook files, but that subject is far beyond our current scope.

When you modify the structure of your worksheet, for example by adding or deleting rows or columns, the absolute cell references will be updated to refer to their new locations in the modified worksheet. They will still work "as advertised" from their new absolute locations.

THE BOTTOM LINE
- The default cell reference in Excel is relative, such as =A1.
- Absolute references are indicated by the $ symbol, such as =$A$1.
- Column, row, and both column and row references can be absolute, as in =$A$1, =$A1, and =A$1.
- The **F4** key is a shortcut to changing cell references from relative to absolute and back.
- Relative references index or increment when cell contents containing cell references are copied to new locations.
- Absolute references do not index or increment, but are updated when the worksheet structure is modified.
- References to other worksheet tabs include the worksheet tab title and an exclamation point (!).
- You can include a pointer or reference to another workbook file by inserting the file name in square brackets, e.g. ([filename]), but these pointers will not work automatically unless both worksheets are currently open.

Setting Up a Data Structure

You can enter information into a cell of a worksheet in two different ways. You already saw one of these: just type information directly into the cells of the worksheet or select the cell and then click to type in the Formula Bar. As a useful alternative, you can also use Excel's default data form, which is a timesaver if you have lots of data entry to do. Assume that you have three test scores for each of five individuals (see Table 1-1) and want to enter this information into your worksheet for further analysis. Before you enter the data, set up a data structure with a row of column headings (variable names). Detailed instructions for setting up the data structure and entering the data follow. The reader who is new to Excel will want to open an Excel workbook file and follow along.

Table 1-1. Example data

Name	Test1	Test2	Test3
Lyle	88	92	89
Jorge	78	62	78
Kim	34	87	62
Frances	76	82	32
Tomeca	66	88	64

Set up the data structure by typing the column headings in Row 1 as shown in Figure 1-16. Use only letters, numbers, and underscores in your column headings, and keep the headings as brief as possible. Begin the heading with a letter. A bottom border (found under **Home > Font**) provides visual separation between the column headings and the data entries.

If you desire visual separation in your labels, you can use a label such as Test_1. As previously discussed, to enter the data in the cells beneath the column headings, you can simply point to the cell with the mouse and click to select the cell or use the arrow keys to navigate from cell to cell. Begin typing, and information is displayed in the cell and the Formula Bar window simultaneously. As soon as you press <**Enter**> or <**Tab**> or simply select another cell, the information you typed into the cell or the Formula Bar will appear in both places. If you are entering formulas, functions, or cell pointers, after the information is entered, the Formula Bar will display the Formula View while the cell will display the result of its application (Value View).

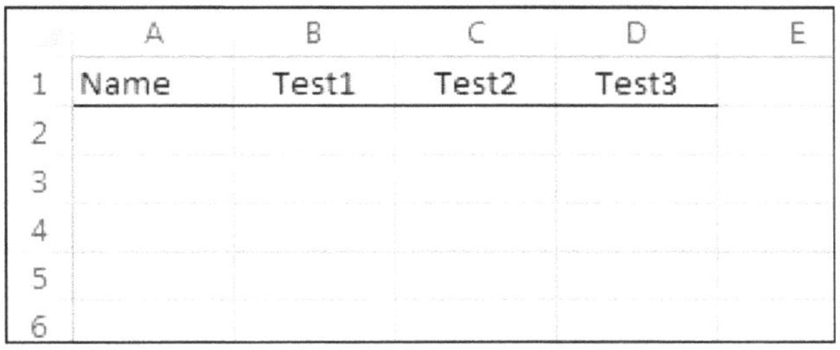

	A	B	C	D	E
1	Name	Test1	Test2	Test3	
2					
3					
4					
5					
6					

Figure 1-16. Data structure with column headings

THE BOTTOM LINE
- Column headings should be as brief as possible.
- Avoid spaces in your column headings.
- Headings should contain only letters, numbers, and underscores. You should begin a heading with a letter.
- You can enter information directly into a cell or into the Formula Bar.

Error Indicators

Sometimes you might accidentally instruct Excel to do something that it does not know how to do, for example, by misspelling the name of a function or entering an invalid range name. If that is the case, Excel will display #NAME? in the affected cell(s). If you try to divide by zero, Excel will give you a #DIV/0 error indicator. Other error indicators in Excel include #N/A, #NULL, #NUM, #REF, and #VALUE. The interested reader should consult the Excel help files for explanations.

Sizing Columns

On other occasions, the information in a cell could be perfectly acceptable, but may require too much space to display correctly in the narrow default column width of 8.43 characters. When that is the case, the information displays as ###### (see Figure 1-17). This is very easy to fix. You can select one or more the columns by clicking in the row of column labels (A, B, C, etc.). Clicking and dragging will select adjacent columns. You can also select nonadjacent columns by holding down <**Ctrl**> and clicking on the column letter. After selecting a column or columns, click the right mouse button and select "Column Width." Entering a larger number will expand the column, and entering a smaller number will shrink it. You can also gain access to column width formatting by selecting **Home > Cells > Format**.

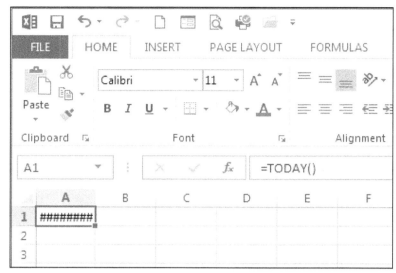

Figure 1-17. Default column is not wide enough to display the result of the Today() function.

You can also more directly and simply click and drag the right column border to expand or shrink the column width. Move the cursor into the row of column labels (A, B, C, etc.) and see that when the pointer is near the right border of a column, the cursor shape changes from a downward pointing arrow (for clicking and selecting the entire column) to a vertical line with double-pointing (left-right) arrows (Figure 1-18). At that point, you can hold down the left mouse button and shrink or expand the column width by dragging the mouse to the left or right. When you use this technique, Excel displays to the right and slightly above the left-right arrow the column width in its own character units and in pixels when you hold down the mouse button.

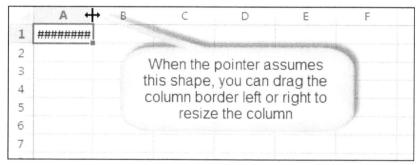

Figure 1-18.

If you double click the left mouse button when the cursor is the vertical line with the double-pointing arrow, the column will automatically resize to fit the contents of the widest cell entry in the column. This AutoFit "auto-widens" and "auto-shrinks" when either there is not enough room for the contents or there is more room than necessary to display the contents. AutoFit also works when you type numbers or dates directly into a cell or when you reformat them. If the typed or formatted entry is too wide, Excel will widen the column accordingly when you press **<Enter>**. If you change a number or shrink the column width, Excel will display as much of the number's decimals as it can. If you type a larger number than the column can accommodate, Excel will report the number in scientific notation. However, the AutoFit feature does not automatically resize columns when you type in text or apply a function or formula to a cell. If you have a column with blank cells to the right, say a column with a long title but narrower typical entries, you can also size the column to the width of the content in the active cell by selecting **Home > Cells > Format > AutoFit Column Width**.

Note in the upper left corner of the worksheet area (to the left of A and above 1) the little rectangle with a triangle in it directly beneath the Name Box (see Figure 1-1). If you click that rectangle, you will select the entire worksheet. After you select the entire sheet, you can right-click to copy it, delete it, clear its contents, or format the entire sheet's cell contents. When the entire worksheet is selected, you can also use the trick just mentioned to resize all the columns of the worksheet by double-clicking on any column border. This device also works to resize the heights of the rows in the worksheet. A little practice with column and row formatting will make your worksheets both more attractive and more effective. In Chapter 2, you will complete the discussion of setting up an effective data structure and talk about some basic descriptive statistics. For now, examine the completed worksheet with all the data entered (see Figure 1-19).

	A	B	C	D
1	Name	Test1	Test2	Test3
2	Lyle	88	92	89
3	Jorge	78	82	78
4	Kim	34	87	62
5	Frances	76	82	32
6	Tomeca	66	88	64
7				

Figure 1-19. Completed data entry

THE BOTTOM LINE
- Excel displays various cell-content error indicator messages that begin with the pound sign (#). Consult the Excel help files for an explanation of error indicators.
- The ######## indicator means that the default column (8.43 characters) or a column of any width is too narrow to display the cell contents properly.
- Column widths can be changed by several methods, including double-clicking on the right cell border to expand or contract the column to fit the widest cell entry. This is called AutoFit.
- AutoFit also works when you type or format numbers and dates to expand the column width. AutoFit does not automatically resize columns when you type text.
- You can also use AutoFit to size a column to an individual cell's content by selecting the cell and then selecting **Home > Cells > Format > AutoFit Column Width**.
- You can select multiple columns by clicking and dragging in the column labels (A, B, C, etc.). You can select nonadjacent columns by **<Ctrl>** + click.
- You can select the entire worksheet and format all its columns and rows at once.

A Date with a Helpful Function

In addition to statistical functions, there are other helpful functions in Excel. People often include dates in their spreadsheets. To Excel, a date is a special kind of number, and dates are stored as numbers by the program and then formatted as dates. Excel has several built-in date formats. There is no further discussion of the technical aspects of dates here, but Excel can perform interesting and useful operations on dates, just as it can with other kinds of numbers. One of the most useful Excel functions is the one called TODAY() that was shown earlier. If you simply type =TODAY(), leaving the parentheses blank, in any empty cell, Excel will display the current date. The date will change to the current date whenever you open the workbook. As we discussed above, the cell width may need to be increased to display the results correctly. Double-clicking on the sizing icon discussed previously instantly widens the column, and the results appear in Figure 1-20 below.

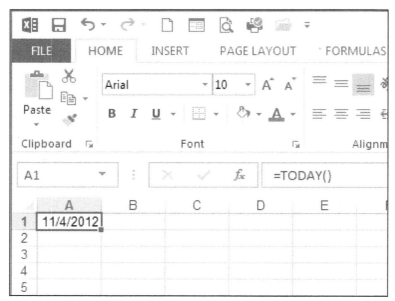

Figure 1-20. Using the TODAY() function to insert the current date in a worksheet

THE BOTTOM LINE

- Excel provides basic arithmetic operators for addition (+), subtraction (−), multiplication (*), division (/), and exponentiation (^).
- These operators are evaluated left to right in a cell.
- Excel also provides operators for negation (−) and percent (%). These are evaluated first.
- The order of operations in Excel is parentheses, exponentiation, multiplication, division, addition, and subtraction.
- The order of operations can be forced by the use of parentheses.
- Other useful functions include SUM, AVERAGE, SQRT, and DEVSQ.
- A list of other statistical functions appears in Appendix A.
- Dates are stored as numbers in Excel.
- The TODAY() function returns the current date.

Chapter 1 Exercises

1. Launch Excel 2010 to reveal a blank workbook file. Type the information shown in Figure 1-19 exactly as it appears. Click on the **File Tab** and click **Save As**. Accept the default Excel workbook format. Type the name "Chapter1" without the quotes. Excel will supply the default ".xlsx" extension. Note that your file now appears in the Recent Documents pane when you click on the **File** Tab. Close Excel. Launch Excel. Open the workbook file you just created by clicking on its name in the Recent Documents list. Select the range B1:B6 and give it the name "Test1" without the quotes. Click on the dropdown arrow in the Name Box to access the range and observe what happens.

2. Give the range A1:A6 the name "Names." Give the range A2:D2 the name "Lyle." Give the range A1:D6 the name "Scores." (Obviously, you should not include the quotes when you type the names. Click on the dropdown arrow to access all the ranges you have created. Observe what

happens when you click on each name. Click **Formulas** and in the **Defined Names** group, click on **Name Manager**. Explore the features in this dialog and then click **Close**.

3. Use Excel's math operators to find answers to the following simple problems. Simply type the necessary data and enter the required formula or function in the blank cells of an Excel worksheet. Try using cell references instead of the actual values in your formulas and functions. Label your worksheet by using appropriately descriptive text entries in the cells adjacent to the cells displaying the answers. Save your worksheet with an appropriate name.

    a. What is 999 divided by 222?
    b. What is 621 + 2443 + 12232 + 1232?
    c. Find the square root of 325351.
    d. What is 33 to the fourth power?
    e. Calculate the sum of the scores for Test1 in your example spreadsheet (see Figure 1-14).
    f. Calculate the average score for Test1 in the example spreadsheet.
    g. What is the average test score for Kim in the example spreadsheet?

4. Open a new workbook file and enter =TODAY() in cell A1. Observe the result. Resize the cell as necessary.

2 Tables and Descriptive Statistics

In this chapter, you complete the discussion from Chapter 1 about data structuring and explore the basic descriptive statistical functions of Excel. Chapter 2 topics include:

- The Table feature (an enhancement of the Data List introduced in Excel 2003).
- Additional statistical functions and tools in Excel.
- The Status Bar.
- Installing the Analysis ToolPak and using the Descriptive Statistics tool.
- Using Excel to find percentiles and percentile ranks.

You learn how to format data as a table and how to use simple formulas and various built-in functions to find descriptive statistics. Next, you learn how to get the most common descriptive statistics for one or more variables at once using the Descriptive Statistics tool in the Analysis ToolPak. Last, you learn how to find percentiles and percentile ranks in Excel.

Working with Structured Data

As discussed in Chapter 1, best practice is to enter a row of column headings that provide labels for the fields (variables) in your worksheet. Look back at the column headings in Figure 1-19 (page 23). These labels provide information about the data entered in the worksheet. Although you may be tempted to enter long labels for the columns and use spaces in your headings, you should avoid this for statistical applications. To keep your workbook manageable, and for the labels to be most effective, you should anticipate that you will also use the labels for range names. Thus, you should keep the labels relatively short and use only letters and numbers in your data labels. As a reminder, the labels should begin with a letter, and should contain only letters, numbers, and underscores. Following these conventions for labeling your variables makes it possible for programs like Minitab, R, and SPSS to import the row of column headings from Excel as variable names.

With Excel 2003, Microsoft introduced a feature called the Data List that made it easier to work with structured information. This feature is now simply called a table in Excel 2010. Although it is possible to sort and filter without using tables, tables make it both easier and safer to use these procedures. Sorting one column without a data list or table destroys the relationship between the fields and records in other columns (I learned this lesson the hard way by ruining more than one data set), but the table keeps all the fields and records together when the records are sorted on one or more fields.

The table tool is in the **Tables** group found on the **Insert** ribbon. Select the entire range or just the upper left cell of the data table and click **Insert** > **Tables** > **Table**. The **Tables** group also provides access to a tool called the PivotTable, which will be discussed in more detail in the next chapter. You can also easily select any range of cells or allow Excel to select all contiguous data in a given worksheet area and convert it to a formatted table using a predefined style from **Home** > **Styles** > **Format as Table**. If you do not highlight the entire range of cells, Excel will try to identify all the contiguous data as part of the table. Once you have created a table, you will have access to the **Table Tools** > **Design** ribbon, where you have a gallery of table styles from which to choose. If you are not a fan of predefined styles, you can also clear the formatting by selecting **Table Tools > Design > Table Styles**. Click on the "More" arrow in the **Table Styles** group (see Figure 2-1). In the resulting new window, select **Clear** at the bottom.

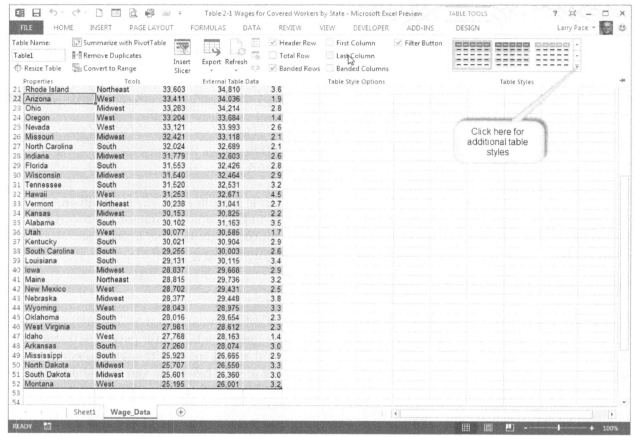

Figure 2-1. Accessing additional visual styles for a table

To convert a table back to a normal range, select **Table Tools > Tools > Convert to Range**.

THE BOTTOM LINE

- The Table feature is an extension of the Excel 2003 Data List.
- To be most effective, tables should be based on the data structuring procedure outlined previously, and should include a row of column headings.
- To create a table with default formatting, select the upper left cell of the data and then choose **Insert > Tables > Table**.
- You can also format data as a table by selecting **Home > Styles > Format as Table** and then selecting one of the gallery styles.
- Each table in the workbook is given a name by Excel and the name appears in the Name Box's dropdown list as well as in the Name Manager.
- When you create a table, you will have a **Table Tools** menu with a **Design** ribbon with **Properties**, **Tools**, **External Table Data**, **Table Style Options**, and **Table Styles** groups.
- To reveal the **Table Tools** menu when it is not visible, click inside the table or select the table name from the Name Box.
- To clear all the table formatting, you can select **Table Tools > Design > Table Styles**, click on the bottom arrow, and then select **Clear**.

- To change a table back to a regular range, select **Table Tools > Tools > Convert to Range**.

More Built-In Functions and Tools

Let us begin the exploration of Excel's additional functions and tools with a tool called AutoSum. Return to the worksheet you created in Chapter 1. You can retrieve a new copy from the companion web page, or you can practice your Excel skills and recreate the file. Add an empty column labeled "PersonAvg" for the individual averages and an empty row labeled "TestAvg" for the test averages (see Figure 2-2). Select the entire range of data including the empty row beneath and empty column to the right to the data. To compute the averages for all three tests and all five people, continue with the AutoSum feature.

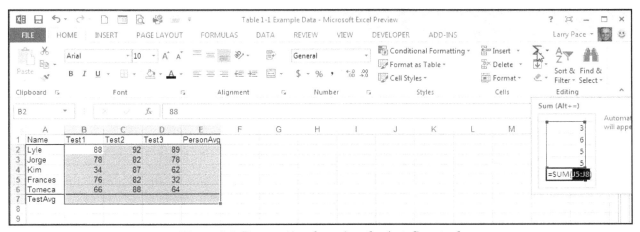

Figure 2-2. Preparation for using the AutoSum tool

From the **Home** ribbon, locate the **Editing** group. Then, click on the dropdown arrow beside the **AutoSum** icon (**Home > Editing > AutoSum**). From the dropdown list, select **Average,** and all the averages will be calculated at the same time (see Figure 2-2). After calculating them, you should format the averages to a single decimal place. Recall from the previous chapter that you can change the number format of a selected cell or cells by clicking on the Launch Dialog button at the bottom right of the **Number** group, or by clicking on the dropdown arrow next to the word General (the default format) in the **Number** group and selecting **Number** (see Figure 2-3). You can also format decimals by selecting the Increase/Decrease Decimal tools (**Home > Number > Increase Decimal**) (Figure 2-4). Finally, in the context-sensitive menu that appears when you right-click in a cell, you can also select **Format > Cells > Number** and change the number of decimal places to whatever you like. In general, the average should be reported with at the least one more significant digit than the raw data, so for integers, the average should have at least one decimal place.

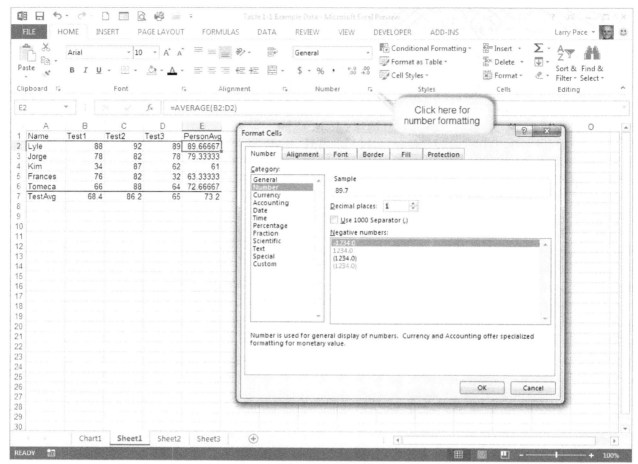

Figure 2-3. Results of using the AutoSum tool and accessing number format options

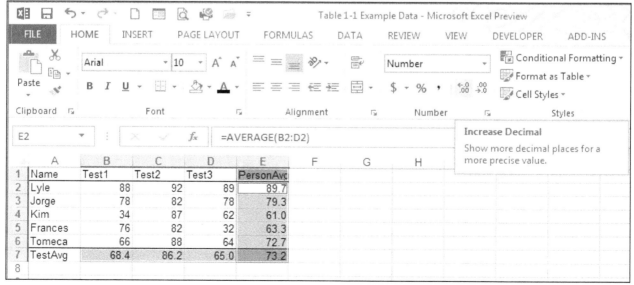

Figure 2-4. Using the Increase Decimal tool

The Formula View

As you have seen, when you enter a function or a formula in a cell or in the Formula Bar, the function or formula displays in the Formula Bar while the result of applying the function or formula appears in the cell itself. That is the normal behavior of Excel. You can click on a cell with a formula, function, or cell pointer in it, and immediately see the cell's function or formula in the Formula Bar. To view all the formulas in the cells of your worksheet at once, press the **<Ctrl>** key and the grave accent (`` ` ``). This key is usually located at the top left of the keyboard under the tilde (~) to the left of the 1 key on most keyboards. Figure 2-5 shows that Excel used the `=AVERAGE(Range)` function to compute the means using relative cell references. Pressing **<Ctrl>** + `` ` `` returns the worksheet to the normal Value View.

	A	B	C	D	E
1	Name	Test1	Test2	Test3	PersonAvg
2	Lyle	88	92	89	=AVERAGE(B2:D2)
3	Jorge	78	82	78	=AVERAGE(B3:D3)
4	Kim	34	87	62	=AVERAGE(B4:D4)
5	Frances	76	82	32	=AVERAGE(B5:D5)
6	Tomeca	66	88	64	=AVERAGE(B6:D6)
7	TestAvg	=AVERAGE(B2:B6)	=AVERAGE(C2:C6)	=AVERAGE(D2:D6)	=AVERAGE(B7:D7)
8					

Figure 2-5. The Formula View. Press <Ctrl> + ` to toggle between Value and Formula Views

---

THE BOTTOM LINE
- The default view of a worksheet is the Value View in which values display in the worksheet area and the formula or function for the active cell displays in the Formula Bar.
- To change to the Formula View in order to see all the functions and formulas in a worksheet at the same time, enter **<Ctrl>** + `` ` ``.
- Entering **<Ctrl>** + `` ` `` a second time will return to the Value View.

Summary Statistics Available From the AutoSum Tool

The AutoSum Tool does more than simply add or average numbers. By default, it provides summary statistics for a selected range of cells. As illustrated above, to activate the AutoSum tool, select the range of cells with a blank cell, row, and/or column for the output. From the **Home** ribbon, click on the **AutoSum** icon to get the sum, or click the adjacent dropdown arrow and select the desired statistic:

- *Sum*
- *Average*
- *Count*
- *Minimum*
- *Maximum*
- *More Functions* (this gives access to the complete function library)

Setting up a Table

As discussed previously, you can create a table with default formatting. To do so, select the desired range of data including the row of column headings, or simply click in the upper left cell of the contiguous data, and then click on **Insert > Tables > Table** (or enter **<Ctrl> + T**) (Figure 2-6). You can also select **Home > Styles > Format as Table** to create a table with a format from the gallery of styles.

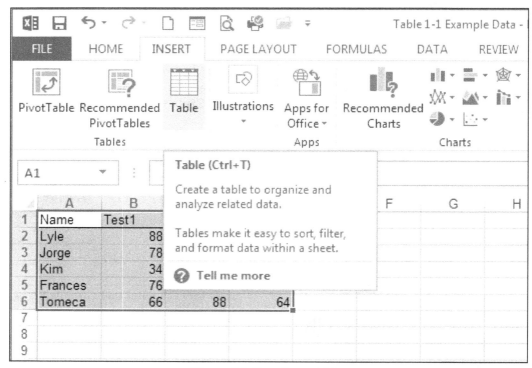

Figure 2-6. Creating a table

The completed table with default formatting is shown in Figure 2-7. The **Table Tools** group with a **Design** tab will now appear in the ribbon whenever the table is selected. Tables allow the user easily to sort, filter, and summarize the data within a selected range of a worksheet. As mentioned previously, the table is a special named object, and the name Table1 will be automatically given to the table you just created. You can see the name and access the table from anywhere in the workbook, even from a different worksheet, by clicking on the dropdown arrow at the right end of the Name Box, and selecting Table1. When you select another worksheet or select a cell outside the table, the **Table Tools** menu and the **Design** tab will disappear from view and will not be visible again until you click inside the table or select the table from the Name Box.

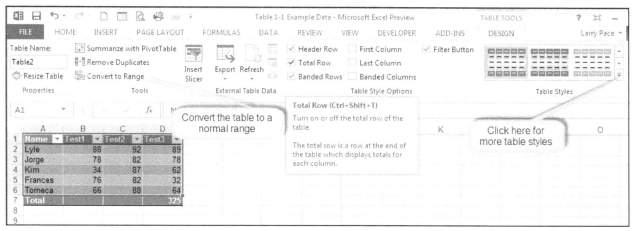

Figure 2-7. Table with default formatting and Total Row added

It is often helpful to add a **Total Row** to your table to give access to the summary statistics and any other built-in functions for each variable (column) in the table. To add a Total Row, click anywhere inside the table. On the **Design** ribbon, select **Total Row (Table Tools > Design > Table Style Options > Total Row)** (see Figure 2-7). By default, Excel will assume that you want to sum the last column of data in the table. You can add statistics for other columns, and you can modify or delete the function applied to the last column or any other column(s). You also turn the **Total Row** off or turn it back on from the **Table Tools > Design > Table Style Options** group. Any of the listed statistics or functions can be chosen for any given variable in the table.

When the data in your table are filtered, the selected summary statistics in the **Total Row** are updated to refer to only the selected values, making the table an excellent way to explore group differences. In statistics, it is useful to set the **Total Row** summary to **Average** for quantitative variables and **Count** for qualitative variables. This is a convenient way to count categories and to summarize numerical data for the entire table and for selected groups of data. As a reminder, if you decide you would like your table to be converted back to a normal range of cells, you can click on the table name in the Name Box to select the table (or simply click anywhere in the table). On the **Table Tools > Design** ribbon in the **Tools** group, click **Convert to Range** and follow the instructions for reverting the table to a normal range (see Figure 2-7).

Excel has a built-in set of table styles, and the user can easily change the table formatting from the **Table Tools** group. Tables with appropriately labeled column headers have an additional advantage. Examine Figure 2-8, which shows the data from Table 2-1 (page 56) formatted as a table (these data are available from the companion web page). Note that when the table is too big to fit on a single screen, the row of column headings replaces the default column labels A, B, C. This makes it very easy to know which column of data you are working with in a large table.

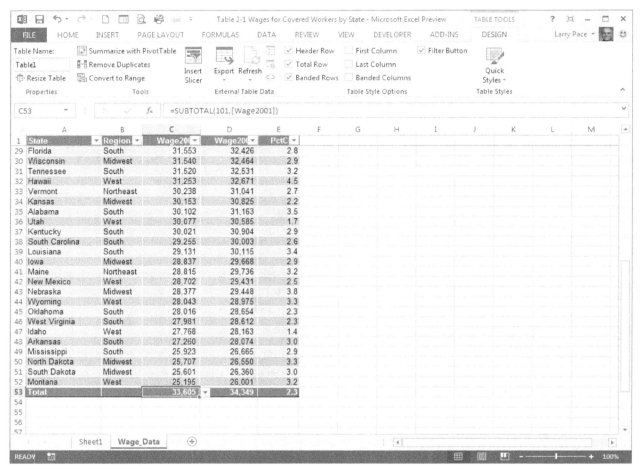

Figure 2-8. Table freezes column headings instead of showing only default column labels (partial data)

Customizing the Status Bar

Unlike the ribbon, the Status Bar can be customized (see Figure 2-9). To gain access to the customization options, right click in the Status Bar on any of the currently displayed features such as the Ready mode indicator in the lower left-hand corner of the worksheet. You can check or uncheck the various features to be displayed in the Status Bar, some of which apply to the worksheet, and some of which apply to only a selected range. For example, if you turn on the Caps Lock, the status indicator in the customization dialog will change from Off to On. If you click in front of Caps Lock, the Caps Lock indicator will now show on the Status Bar. Summary statistics such as Average, Count, Minimum, Maximum, and Sum will show only when numerical data are selected. It is not necessary to use either tables or named ranges for these statistics to display and to change when the selected data change.

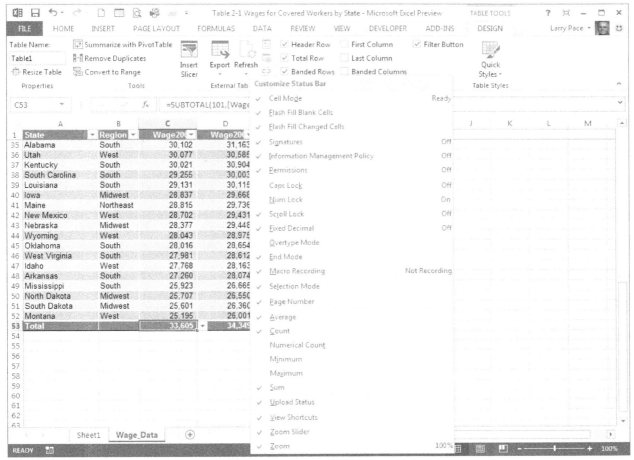

Figure 2-9. Options for customizing the Status Bar

Additional Statistical Functions

As a reminder, to add a **Total Row**, you should click inside the table, or select its name in the Name Box. Then from the **Table Tools** group's **Design** ribbon, select **Total Row**. The table with a **Total Row** added is shown in Figure 2-10. Note that you can use any of the supplied functions and click on **More Functions** to gain access to the function library.

	A	B	C	D	E	F
1	**State** ▼	**Region** ▼	**Wage200** ▼	**Wage200** ▼	**PctC** ▼	
35	Alabama	South	30,102	31,163	3.5	
36	Utah	West	30,077	30,585	1.7	
37	Kentucky	South	30,021	30,904	2.9	
38	South Carolina	South	29,255	30,003	2.6	
39	Louisiana	South	29,131	30,115	3.4	
40	Iowa	Midwest	28,837	29,668	2.9	
41	Maine	Northeast	28,815	29,736	3.2	
42	New Mexico	West	28,702	29,431	2.5	
43	Nebraska	Midwest	28,377	29,448	3.8	
44	Wyoming	West	28,043	28,975	3.3	
45	Oklahoma	South	28,016	28,654	2.3	
46	West Virginia	South	27,981	28,612	2.3	
47	Idaho	West	27,768	28,163	1.4	
48	Arkansas	South	27,260	28,074	3.0	
49	Mississippi	South	25,923	26,665	2.9	
50	North Dakota	Midwest	25,707	26,550	3.3	
51	South Dakota	Midwest	25,601	26,360	3.0	
52	Montana	West	25,195	26,001	3.2	
53	**Total**		**33,605** ▼	**34,349**	**2.3**	
54			None			
55			Average			
56			Count			
57			Count Numbers			
58			Max			
59			Min			
60			Sum			
61			StdDev			
			Var			
62			More Functions...			

Figure 2-10. Table with Total Row added

As an alternative or an addition to using a **Total Row** or the **Status Bar**, you can get to Excel's built-in statistical functions via the **Insert Function** command. This command is always available by clicking on the *fx* symbol to the left of the Formula Bar. You can also select the **Formulas** tab, locate the **Function Library** group, and then select **Insert Function** as shown in Figure 2-11. Click on the dropdown arrow next to **More Functions** icon in the **Function Library** group and click on **Statistical (Formulas > Function Library > More Functions**). A partial list of the statistical functions available in Excel 2010, 2011, and 2013 is displayed in Figure 2-12.

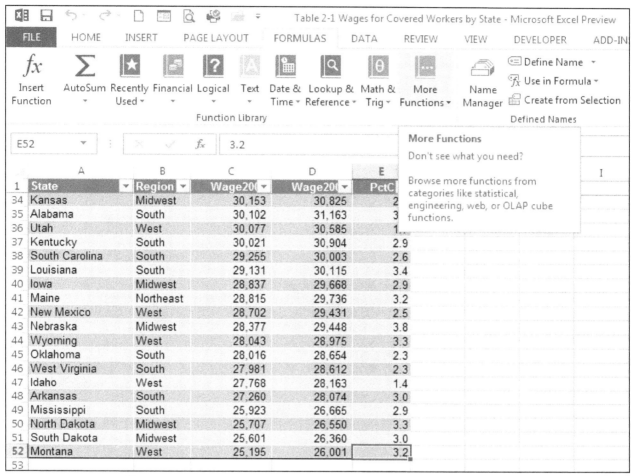

Figure 2-11. Function Library group reveals the More Functions icon

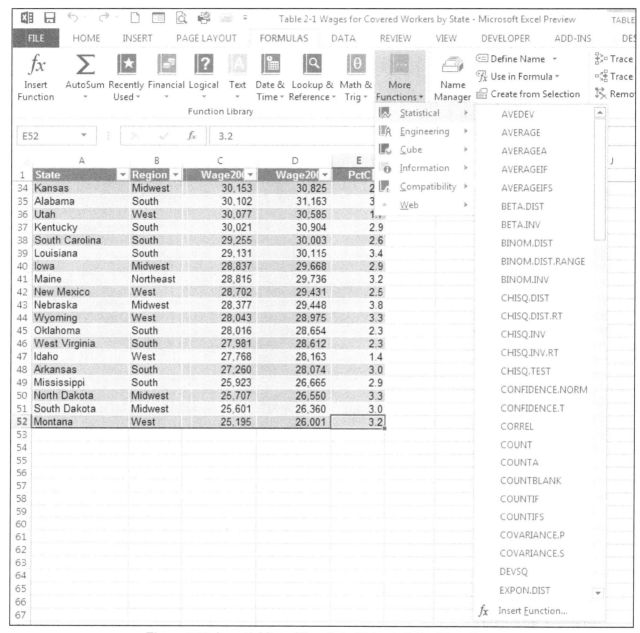

Figure 2-12. A partial list of Excel's built-in statistical functions

Clicking on the **Insert Function** icon or on any of the function names in the Function Library will launch a dialog with a help feature that allows you to enter the arguments. Selecting from menus and dialogs is helpful for learning the functions and how to use them, but you will soon remember the names of the functions you use most often. It is easy to bypass all the extra pointing and clicking to access a function. For example, once know the name of the DEVSQ function for calculating the sum of squares, you can simply go to a blank cell in your worksheet, and type

=DEVSQ(

Then, after the open left parenthesis, enter the actual values, cell references, or the name of the desired range of values. When you close the parentheses and press <**Enter**>, Excel will automatically calculate the sum of squares. Appendix A of this book contains a list of many of the most commonly used statistical functions. Throughout the book, you will learn to type the name of the function for immediate access to it rather than to use the menu-driven interface. This will save you a lot of pointing and clicking in the end, and is worth the extra effort to learn.

THE BOTTOM LINE

- The AutoSum tool is located under **Home** > **Editing** > **AutoSum**. Clicking the icon produces the sum. The dropdown menu next to the icon gives access to the various additional functions.
- This tool allows the user to find the sum, average, count, minimum, and maximum values in a selected data range. Clicking **More Functions** opens the function library.
- Adding a Total Row to a table also provides access to various summary statistics for the columns of data in the table, as well as to the function Library.
- To add a Total Row, select the table name from the Name Box or select any cell in the table and then select **Table Tools** > **Design** > **Table Style Options** > **Total Row**.
- You can also gain access to the function library by clicking on the *fx* (**Insert Function** icon) at the left of the Formula Bar, or by selecting **Formulas** > **Function Library** > **Insert Function**.

Installing the Analysis ToolPak

Many Excel add-ins and macros provide increased or specialized statistical functionality. In order to keep things both as simple and as general as possible, this book avoids macros entirely, and is concerned with only one add-in, the Analysis ToolPak provided by Microsoft. If you are a user of Excel 2008 or 2011 for Mac, the Analysis ToolPak is not available to you. However, you can use a similar tool (also freely available) called StatPlus:mac LE:

```
http://www.analystsoft.com/en/products/statplusmacle/
```

Users of Excel 2011 for Mac can also install the statistics add-in MegaStat, which is discussed and illustrated in Appendix D of this book.

The Analysis ToolPak comes with Excel for Windows, but is not installed by default. To install the Analysis ToolPak, click the **File** tab, and then click the **Options** button located at the bottom of the dialog box (see Figure 2-13). Click **Add-ins**, and then in the **Manage** box, select **Excel Add-ins**. Click **Go**. In next box, select "Manage Excel Add-ins" and then click **Go** (see Figure 2-14).

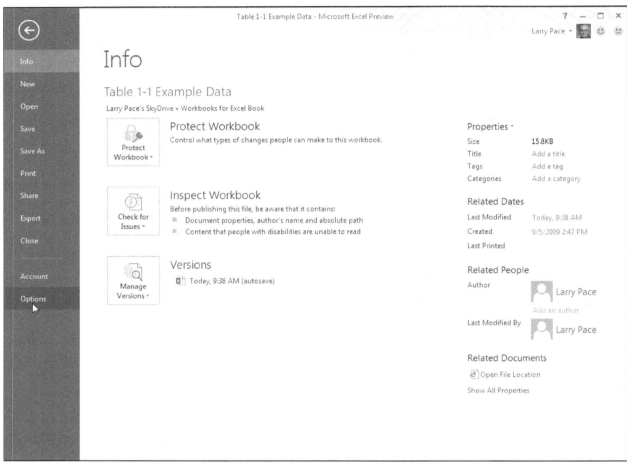

Figure 2-13. Accessing Excel options

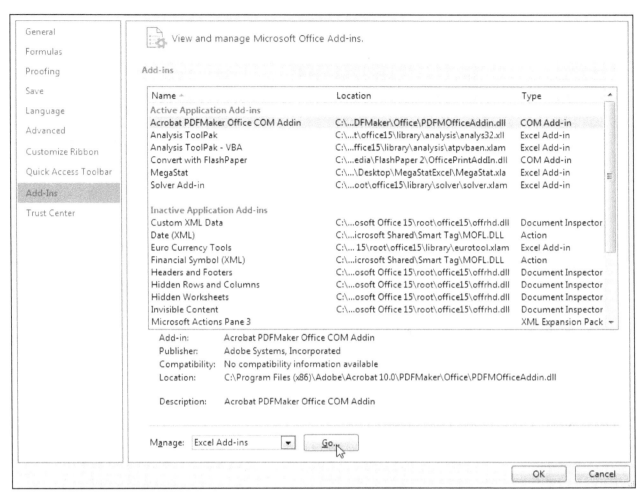

Figure 2-14. Select "Manage Excel Add-ins" and then click Go

Now, check the box in front of "Analysis ToolPak" (see Figure 2-15). Click **OK**.

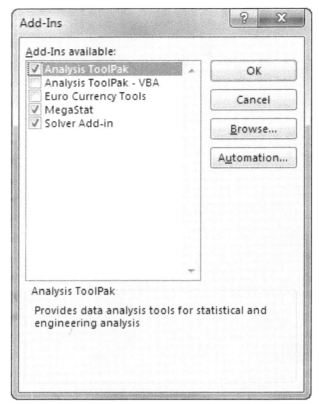

Figure 2-15. Enabling the Analysis ToolPak add-in

After you have installed the Analysis ToolPak, there will be a **Data Analysis** tool available via the **Analysis** group under the **Data** ribbon (**Data > Analysis > Data Analysis**). See Figure 2-16. Unlike the built-in functions or formulas in the cells of a worksheet, add-ins like the Analysis ToolPak produce static output. As discussed previously, if you change a data value or values in the worksheet, the results of any associated formulas and functions will update dynamically. However, with the Analysis ToolPak, when you change one or more data values or add more data, you will have to run the procedure again to update the results.

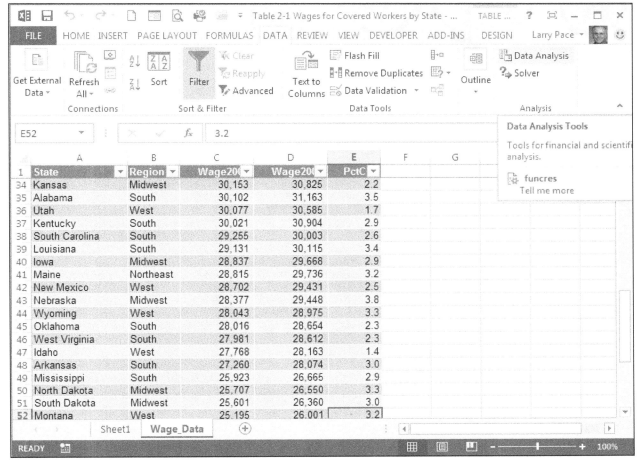

Figure 2-16. Analysis group and Data Analysis tool icon added to Data ribbon

Example Data

Table 2-1 presents the average wages for all covered workers in the 50 states and the District of Columbia) for the years 2001 and 2002 (source: U.S. Bureau of Labor Statistics, http://www.bls.gov/cew/state2002.txt). These data have already been illustrated in the screen captures in the previous sections of this chapter. You can retrieve these data from the companion web page.

Table 2-1. Average wages for all covered workers by state or district, 2001 and 2002

State	Region	Wage2001	Wage2002	PctChg	State	Region	Wage2001	Wage2002	PctChg
Alabama	South	30,102	31,163	3.525	Montana	West	25,195	26,001	3.199
Alaska	West	36,170	37,134	2.665	Nebraska	Midwest	28,377	29,448	3.774
Arizona	West	33,411	34,036	1.871	Nevada	West	33,121	33,993	2.633
Arkansas	South	27,260	28,074	2.986	New Hampshire	Northeast	35,481	36,176	1.959
California	West	41,327	41,419	0.223	New Jersey	Northeast	44,320	45,182	1.945
Colorado	West	37,952	38,005	0.140	New Mexico	West	28,702	29,431	2.540
Connecticut	Northeast	46,993	46,852	-0.300	New York	Northeast	46,727	46,328	-0.854
Delaware	South	38,427	39,684	3.271	North Carolina	South	32,024	32,689	2.077
District of Columbia	South	55,908	57,914	3.588	North Dakota	Midwest	25,707	26,550	3.279
Florida	South	31,553	32,426	2.767	Ohio	Midwest	33,283	34,214	2.797
Georgia	South	35,136	35,734	1.702	Oklahoma	South	28,016	28,654	2.277
Hawaii	West	31,253	32,671	4.537	Oregon	West	33,204	33,684	1.446
Idaho	West	27,768	28,163	1.423	Pennsylvania	Northeast	34,978	35,808	2.373
Illinois	Midwest	39,083	39,688	1.548	Rhode Island	Northeast	33,603	34,810	3.592
Indiana	Midwest	31,779	32,603	2.593	South Carolina	South	29,255	30,003	2.557
Iowa	Midwest	28,837	29,668	2.882	South Dakota	Midwest	25,601	26,360	2.965
Kansas	Midwest	30,153	30,825	2.229	Tennessee	South	31,520	32,531	3.207
Kentucky	South	30,021	30,904	2.941	Texas	South	36,045	36,248	0.563
Louisiana	South	29,131	30,115	3.378	Utah	West	30,077	30,585	1.689
Maine	Northeast	28,815	29,736	3.196	Vermont	Northeast	30,238	31,041	2.656
Maryland	South	38,253	39,382	2.951	Virginia	South	36,733	37,222	1.331
Massachusetts	Northeast	44,975	44,954	-0.047	Washington	West	37,459	38,242	2.090
Michigan	Midwest	37,391	38,135	1.990	West Virginia	South	27,981	28,612	2.255
Minnesota	Midwest	36,587	37,458	2.381	Wisconsin	Midwest	31,540	32,464	2.930
Mississippi	South	25,923	26,665	2.862	Wyoming	West	28,043	28,975	3.323
Missouri	Midwest	32,421	33,118	2.150					

If you type the data into your own worksheet, the data should be structured as discussed previously, with a row for each state (record) and a column with an appropriate heading for each variable as shown in Figure 2-16. To build the worksheet structure, after selecting the range of all 51 entries for 2001 wages (and including the text label in the range), give the selected range the name "Wage2001" (without the quotes of course) by typing the name into the Name Box. The same should be done for the 2002 wages and the other fields in the worksheet.

As you learned in Chapter 1, you can enter the name of the desired range in an Excel function or formula rather than typing in the range of cell references. Remember it is also easy to select the entire range again by clicking on its name in the Name Box. It makes much more sense to another user of your workbook to see a function that says

```
=AVERAGE(Wage2001)
```

than it does to see one that says

```
=AVERAGE(C2:C52)
```

It is not technically necessary to put all the data in a single column to apply many Excel functions. You could have a multicolumn table and name a range of data that is a matrix rather than an array. However, you will find it harder after that to do anything else with the specific columns of data. Good form is to use a single row for each record and a single column for all the entries in a particular field (variable) unless the multiple columns apply to distinct groups or to distinct fields, such as the wages from two different years as in the current case. Remember that in an Excel 2013 worksheet, you can have a million rows and 16,000 columns, and you can have 255 worksheets in a workbook file, so you are unlikely to run out of space.

> **THE BOTTOM LINE**
> - The Analysis ToolPak provides many statistical tools.
> - To install the Analysis ToolPak, click **File** > **Excel Options** > **Add-ins** > **Manage Excel Add-ins** > **Go**.
> - In the resulting Add-ins dialog, check the box in front of Analysis ToolPak and click **OK**.
> - After installation, the Analysis ToolPak is available via **Data** > **Analysis** > **Data Analysis**.

Freezing Panes

If your worksheet is too large to fit in one screen, you may find it convenient to "freeze" the row of column headings and row labels. That way, when you scroll down in your worksheet, the column headings will stay on the screen. To do this, select **View** > **Window** > **Freeze Panes**. You can freeze the top row, the left column, or all the rows above and columns to the left of a selected cell.

Splitting a Worksheet

When your worksheets grow large, you can "split" the window so that you can look at different sections of the spreadsheet at the same time. You can split the worksheet horizontally, vertically, or both. Slit a worksheet by using the **View** ribbon (**View** > **Window** > **Split**).

Figure 2-17 shows the table with a vertical split. You can scroll separately in each section. In Figure 2-18, the table is shown with both vertical and horizontal splits. As mentioned, you can remove a split by dragging the split control back to its original location. You click **View** > **Window** > **Split** a second time to remove a split.

	B	C	D	E	F
1	Region	Wage2001	Wage2002	PctChg	
2	South	55,908	57,914	3.6	
3	Northeast	46,993	46,852	-0.3	
4	Northeast	46,727	46,328	-0.9	
5	Northeast	44,975	44,954	0.0	
6	Northeast	44,320	45,182	1.9	
7	West	41,327	41,419	0.2	
8	Midwest	39,083	39,688	1.5	
9	South	38,427	39,684	3.3	
10	South	38,253	39,382	3.0	
11	West	37,952	38,005	0.1	
12	West	37,459	38,242	2.1	
43	Midwest	28,377	29,448	3.8	
44	West	28,043	28,975	3.3	
45	South	28,016	28,654	2.3	
46	South	27,981	28,612	2.3	
47	West	27,768	28,163	1.4	
48	South	27,260	28,074	3.0	
49	South	25,923	26,665	2.9	
50	Midwest	25,707	26,550	3.3	
51	Midwest	25,601	26,360	3.0	
52	West	25,195	26,001	3.2	
53		33,605	34,349	2.3	
54					
55					

Figure 2-17. Window with a horizontal split

⊿	A	B	C	D	E	F
1	State	Region	Wage2001	Wage2002	PctChg	
2	District of Columbia	South	55,908	57,914	3.6	
3	Connecticut	Northeast	46,993	46,852	-0.3	
4	New York	Northeast	46,727	46,328	-0.9	
5	Massachusetts	Northeast	44,975	44,954	0.0	
6	New Jersey	Northeast	44,320	45,182	1.9	
7	California	West	41,327	41,419	0.2	
8	Illinois	Midwest	39,083	39,688	1.5	
9	Delaware	South	38,427	39,684	3.3	
10	Maryland	South	38,253	39,382	3.0	
11	Colorado	West	37,952	38,005	0.1	
12	Washington	West	37,459	38,242	2.1	
40	Iowa	Midwest	28,837	29,668	2.9	
41	Maine	Northeast	28,815	29,736	3.2	
42	New Mexico	West	28,702	29,431	2.5	
43	Nebraska	Midwest	28,377	29,448	3.8	
44	Wyoming	West	28,043	28,975	3.3	
45	Oklahoma	South	28,016	28,654	2.3	
46	West Virginia	South	27,981	28,612	2.3	
47	Idaho	West	27,768	28,163	1.4	
48	Arkansas	South	27,260	28,074	3.0	
49	Mississippi	South	25,923	26,665	2.9	
50	North Dakota	Midwest	25,707	26,550	3.3	
51	South Dakota	Midwest	25,601	26,360	3.0	
52	Montana	West	25,195	26,001	3.2	
53	Total		33,605	34,349	2.3	
54						

Figure 2-18. Using both horizontal and vertical splits to see more of the worksheet

---

THE BOTTOM LINE
- You can freeze the top row, the left column, or the rows above and the columns to the left of a selected cell.
- Select **View** > **Window** > **Freeze Panes**.
- You can split a worksheet horizontally or vertically, or both.
- Drag the splits from their default location to the desired location.
- You can also split a worksheet by selecting **View** > **Window** > **Split**. Clicking **View** > **Window** > **Split** again will remove the split.

New to Excel–Better Statistical Functions

Microsoft extended the statistical functionality of Excel with version 2010, and brought Excel up to industry standard with modifications to many of the statistical functions. These enhanced statistical functions are also available in Excel 2011 for Mac and Excel 2013 for Windows. If you are using any previous version of Excel, this is a good reason to upgrade. If you are using Excel 2007 or a previous version, all the "legacy" functions still work in the newer versions of Excel for the sake of backward compatibility, but you should take the time to learn the newest statistical functions in Excel, as they often give superior results. Here is a link to a blog post with more information:

http://blogs.office.com/b/microsoft-excel/archive/2009/09/10/function-improvements-in-excel-2010.aspx

As we discuss the various statistical functions and built-in distributions, I will demonstrate both the newer and the legacy functions.

Using Functions for Descriptive Statistics

First, let us explore some of the built-in statistical functions of Excel. The formulas below use named ranges for the sake of clarity. Various descriptive statistics can be computed and displayed by the use of simple formulas combined with Excel's built-in statistical functions. Excel functions determine and display measures of central tendency (mean, mode, and median), the variance and standard deviation, the minimum and maximum values, the first and third quartiles, percentiles, and many other summary statistics. A list of some of the most common and useful statistical functions in Excel appears in Appendix A.

Table 2-2 shows the Formula View to demonstrate how to use Excel functions and simple formulas to calculate and display common descriptive statistics for both years' wages for all 50 states and the District of Columbia. The Value View is shown in Table 2-3. Named ranges make it clear which variables are being summarized. As discussed earlier, it is possible to enter these functions through the **Function Library** group or other menu-driven approaches, but it is more efficient just to memorize the names (or keep a list nearby) and type them directly into blank cells where you want the results to display in your worksheet.

Table 2-2. Examples of summary statistics (Formula View)

Statistic	2001 Wages	2002 Wages
Minimum	=MIN(Wage2001)	=MIN(Wage2002)
Maximum	=MAX(Wage2001)	=MAX(Wage2002)
Range	=MAX(Wage2001)-MIN(Wage2001)	=MAX(Wage2002)-MIN(Wage2002)
Count	=COUNT(Wage2001)	=COUNT(Wage2002)
Mean	=AVERAGE(Wage2001)	=AVERAGE(Wage2002)
Median	=MEDIAN(Wage2001)	=MEDIAN(Wage2002)
Variance	=VAR.S(Wage2001)	=VAR.S(Wage2002)
Standard Deviation	=STDEV.S(Wage2001)	=STDEV.S(Wage2002)
First Quartile	=QUARTILE.EXC(Wage2001,1)	=QUARTILE.EXC(Wage2002,1)
Third Quartile	=QUARTILE.EXC(Wage2001,3)	=QUARTILE.EXC(Wage2002,3)
Interquartile Range	=B11-B10	=C11-C10
10th Percentile	=PERCENTILE.EXC(Wage2001,0.1)	=PERCENTILE.EXC(Wage2002,0.1)
90th Percentile	=PERCENTILE.EXC(Wage2001,0.9)	=PERCENTILE.EXC(Wage2002,0.9)

Table 2-3. Statistics (Value View) after cell formatting

Statistic	2001 Wages	2002 Wages
Minimum	25195	26001
Maximum	55908	57914
Range	30713	31913
Count	51	51
Mean	33605.08	34348.57
Median	32024	32689
Variance	39234361.67	38627114.77
Standard Deviation	6263.73	6215.07
First Quartile	28837	29736
Third Quartile	36733	37458
Interquartile Range	7896	7722
10th Percentile	27361.60	28091.80
90th Percentile	43721.40	44247.00

After finding the mean and standard deviation, one can use the STANDARDIZE function in Excel to produce z scores for each value of x. Supply the actual values or the cell references for the raw data, the mean, and the standard deviation, and the STANDARDIZE function will calculate the z score for each observation. The subject of z scores and the standard normal distribution is so crucial to statistics that Chapter 4 is devoted to the topic.

Descriptive Statistics in the Analysis ToolPak

The Analysis ToolPak further simplifies and streamlines the computation of the most commonly used descriptive statistics. The Descriptive Statistics tool calculates and displays descriptive statistics instantly for one or more variables. To access this tool, select **Data** > **Analysis** > **Data Analysis** > **Descriptive Statistics**. If you do not see the **Data Analysis** icon in the **Data** ribbon as shown in Figure 2-14, then you must first install the Analysis ToolPak as instructed beginning on page 39. In the Data Analysis dialog, scroll to Descriptive Statistics and click **OK** to launch the Descriptive Statistics dialog. Click in the Input Range field and enter the desired range or range name. If the dialog box is in your way, you can move it, or you can click the little "minimize dialog" icon that resembles a miniature spreadsheet at the right of the field and select the desired range with the mouse or cursor keys. When you press <**Enter**> or click on the "maximize dialog" icon, the dialog box will be restored to full size. The dialog box for the Descriptive Statistics tool is shown in Figure 2-19.

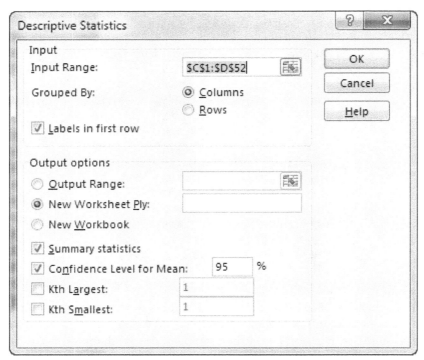

Figure 2-19. Descriptive Statistics tool dialog box

Because there are headings in the first row and the heading was included that row in the selected input range, you should check the box in front of "Labels in first row." If you check labels and you do not have labels, Excel will obediently use the first data value as a label, and your analyses will be incorrect as a result. If you do not have or use labels, Excel will label the output Column1, Column2, Column3, and so on for each included variable. Meaningful labels obviously make the output easier to read and interpret.

The summary output (after some additional cell formatting) tool appears in Table 2-4. You must check at least the box in front of "Summary statistics" for this tool to work. It is also a good idea to check the box in front of "Confidence Level for Mean." The default for a 95% confidence interval is what you usually want, but you can change it to a different value, such as 99% or 90%. What Excel labels the "Confidence Level" is the error margin to be added to and subtracted from the sample mean for a confidence interval for the population mean. We discuss that in more detail later in this chapter.

Table 2-4. Summary output from Descriptive Statistics tool

Wage2001		Wage2002	
Mean	33605.08	Mean	34348.57
Standard Error	877.10	Standard Error	870.28
Median	32024	Median	32689
Mode	#N/A	Mode	#N/A
Standard Deviation	6263.73	Standard Deviation	6215.07
Sample Variance	39234361.67	Sample Variance	38627114.77
Kurtosis	2.26	Kurtosis	3.03
Skewness	1.32	Skewness	1.42
Range	30713	Range	31913
Minimum	25195	Minimum	26001
Maximum	55908	Maximum	57914
Sum	1713859	Sum	1751777
Count	51	Count	51
Confidence Level(95.0%)	1761.70	Confidence Level(95.0%)	1748.02

The legacy CONFIDENCE function in Excel makes use of the standard normal (z) distribution, while the confidence interval reported by the Descriptive Statistics tool makes use of the t distribution on the assumption that the data are a sample and the population parameters are unknown. We will discuss this in more detail shortly. The #N/A displayed for the mode in Table 2.4 indicates that the current data do not have a modal value. When data have more than one mode, Excel will locate and report only the first and lowest value of the mode.

Describing the Descriptive Statistics

Following are brief explanations of the descriptive statistics calculated and displayed by the Descriptive Statistics tool. As mentioned, this tool assumes that the data are a sample from a larger population, and thus reports estimates of the population parameters.

1. The *mean* is calculated as the arithmetic average of the numeric values in the selected range. This function is implemented directly in Excel as AVERAGE(Range).

$$\bar{x} = \frac{\sum x}{n}$$

2. The *standard error* is the standard error of the mean, calculated as follows. There is no intrinsic Excel function for the standard error of the mean, but it is easy to find using the Descriptive Statistics tool.

$$s_{\bar{x}} = \frac{s_x}{\sqrt{n}}$$

3. The *median* is the 50th percentile. It is the observed (always the case for odd-numbered n) or hypothetical (often the case for even-numbered n) found at the location

$$\frac{n+1}{2}$$

in the ordered (sorted from lowest to highest) data set. The Excel function MEDIAN(Range) finds the median. If the number of data points is even, Excel reports the average of the two middle values in the ordered data set as the median.

4. The *mode* is the most frequently occurring value in a data set. Data may have no modal value (see Table 2.4), a single mode, or more than one mode. For multimodal data, Excel finds only the first and lowest value of the mode in the ordered data set. The Excel function is MODE(Range).

5. The sample *standard deviation* is calculated as

$$s_x = \sqrt{\frac{\sum(x-\overline{x})^2}{n-1}}$$

The Excel function for the above index is STDEV.S(Range).

6. The *sample variance* is the square of the standard deviation. The Excel function is VAR.S(Range).

7. *Kurtosis* is an index of the "peakedness" or flatness of the data distribution. Excel returns an estimate of the population kurtosis. The normal distribution by definition has zero kurtosis. Values greater than zero indicate relatively peaked distributions, and negative kurtosis indicates relatively flatter distributions. Kurtosis in Excel is calculated as

$$\left\{\frac{n(n+1)}{(n-1)(n-2)(n-3)}\sum\left(\frac{x-\overline{x}}{s_x}\right)^4\right\}-\frac{3(n-1)^2}{(n-2)(n-3)}$$

The Excel function is KURT(Range).

8. *Skewness* is a measure of the symmetry of the data distribution. Excel returns an estimate of the population skewness. Data may be positively skewed, negatively skewed, or symmetrical (unskewed). The normal distribution has zero skew. Skewness in Excel is calculated as

$$\frac{n}{(n-1)(n-2)}\sum\left(\frac{x-\overline{x}}{s_x}\right)^3$$

The Excel function is SKEW(Range).

9. The *range* is the difference between the maximum and the minimum values. There is no intrinsic function for the range in Excel, but entering any blank cell and typing the following simple formula

=MAX(Range) - Min(Range)

will calculate and display this value.

10. The *maximum* is the largest value in the distribution. The Excel function is `MAX(Range)`.

11. The *minimum* is the smallest value in the distribution. The Excel function is `MIN(Range)`.

12. The *sum* is the total of all the raw data values. The Excel function is `SUM(Range)`.

13. The *count* is the number of all the raw data values, or n. The Excel function is `COUNT(Range)`.

14. As discussed briefly above, the *confidence level* is the "margin of error," one-half the width of a confidence interval for the mean at the specified level of confidence. Note that this value is based on the t distribution rather than the normal distribution, on the assumption that the population standard deviation is unknown. The margin of error is calculated using a two-tailed t value at $n - 1$ degrees of freedom and the desired alpha level (usually .05):

$$t_{\alpha/2}\left(s_{\bar{x}}\right)$$

A confidence interval for the population mean is found as:

$$\bar{x} - t_{\alpha/2}\left(s_{\bar{x}}\right) \leq \mu \leq \bar{x} + t_{\alpha/2}\left(s_{\bar{x}}\right)$$

To illustrate, note that the value of the mean wages for 2001 is \$33,605.08. The standard error is the standard deviation divided by the square root of the sample size:

$$s_{\bar{x}} = \frac{s_x}{\sqrt{n}} = \frac{6263.734}{\sqrt{51}} = \frac{6263.734}{7.141428} = 877.098$$

This value is reported by the Descriptive Statistics tool (see Table 2-4 on page 63). To calculate the margin of error, we note there are $51 - 1 = 50$ degrees of freedom. A critical value of t for an alpha level of .05 and 50 df is found by use of the `T.INV.2T` function (see chapter 5 for details). The critical value is 2.00856. We multiply the standard error by the critical value to determine the margin of error: $877.098 \times 2.00856 = 1761.70$. Add the margin of error to the sample mean to get the upper limit of the confidence interval, and subtract the margin from the sample mean to get the lower limit. This is the confidence interval reported by SPSS and other statistics packages. As a reminder, while the Analysis ToolPak uses the t distribution for confidence intervals, Excel's separate `CONFIDENCE` function uses the standard normal distribution. Because of the large sample size, the two values will be close, and in fact the legacy `CONFIDENCE` function returns a margin of error of 1719.08. In Excel 2010 and newer, this function has been supplanted by `CONFIDENCE.NORM` and `CONFIDENCE.T`, both of which return the margin of error rather than the confidence interval *per se*.

A Note on Samples and Populations

Excel 2010 provides several functions for the variance and the standard deviation. One of these is the commonly used estimator of the population parameter. As discussed above, Excel makes the default assumption that one's data are a sample. The STDEV.S and VAR.S functions make use of an $n - 1$ correction in the denominator of the equation for the variance. These functions use the following formula for the variance (the standard deviation is simply the square root of the variance):

$$s^2 = \frac{\sum (x - \bar{x})^2}{n - 1}$$

To access the sample variance directly, type

=VAR.S(Range)

and for the sample standard deviation,

=STDEV.S(Range)

These are the values reported by the Analysis ToolPak and by most other statistical packages. You can also treat the data as a population, and the mean as the population mean, μ. These functions use n as the denominator in the definitional formula:

$$\sigma^2 = \frac{\sum (x - \mu)^2}{N}$$

where N is the number of elements in the population. In Excel 2010 and newer versions, the population variance is accessed by

=VAR.P(Range)

and the population standard deviation by

=STDEV.P(Range)

It is easy to remember the differences between these functions because P stands for "population" and "parameter," while S stands for "sample" and "statistic." Excel also has functions called STDEVA and STDEVPA. These functions are useful for calculating the sample or population standard deviation when the data range contains text in addition to numerical values, or contains logical values such as True or False. True is evaluated as 1, and False is evaluated as 0. Numbers and logical values are included, but text values are simply ignored in the calculations.

If you have an earlier version of Excel, use VAR for the sample variance, VARP for the population variance, STDEV for the sample standard deviation, and STDEVP for the population standard deviation.

THE BOTTOM LINE

- Summary statistics can be found by using functions and formulas or by use of the Analysis ToolPak.
- The Descriptive Statistics tool is available by selecting **Data > Analysis > Data Analysis > Descriptive Statistics**.
- This tool provides various descriptive statistics and can calculate a margin of error for the population mean estimated from the sample data.
- These statistics assume that the data are a sample, not a population.

> • The confidence level reported by the Descriptive Statistics tool is based on the *t* distribution, while Excel's separate CONFIDENCE function uses the standard normal (*z*) distribution.

Frequency Distributions

You can create both simple and grouped frequency distributions using the FREQUENCY function or the Histogram tool in the Analysis ToolPak. Both approaches are illustrated below. Assume that you asked 24 randomly selected students at Paragon State University how many hours they study each week on average. You collect the following information (see Table 2-5). These data are available from the companion web page.

Table 2-5. Weekly study hours for 24 PSU students (hypothetical data)

5	5	3
2	8	4
6	2	2
2	7	4
5	3	4
4	5	3
2	6	2
5	5	5

As we have discussed, the data should be entered in a single column in Excel, with an appropriate label (see Figure 2-20). The data are entered in Column A. In Column B, type the possible individual *x* values, which are known in Excel terminology as "bins."

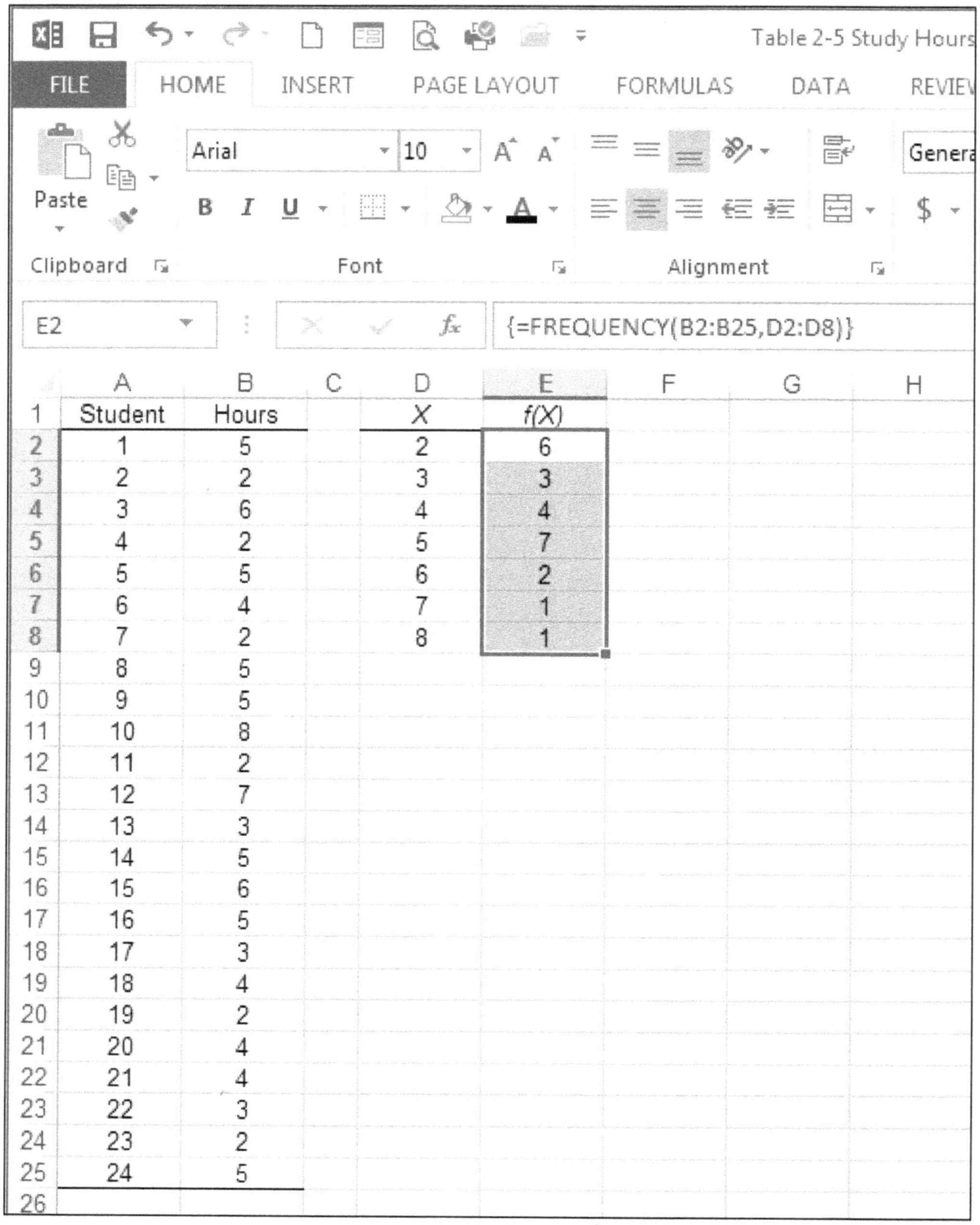

	A	B	C	D	E
1	Student	Hours		X	f(X)
2	1	5		2	6
3	2	2		3	3
4	3	6		4	4
5	4	2		5	7
6	5	5		6	2
7	6	4		7	1
8	7	2		8	1
9	8	5			
10	9	5			
11	10	8			
12	11	2			
13	12	7			
14	13	3			
15	14	5			
16	15	6			
17	16	5			
18	17	3			
19	18	4			
20	19	2			
21	20	4			
22	21	4			
23	22	3			
24	23	2			
25	24	5			

Figure 2-20. Simple frequency distribution in Excel

For a simple frequency distribution, each individual value is a bin. In Column E (see Figure 2-20), Excel displays the frequency of each *x* value in the data set. The frequency distribution in Column C was created via the use of the `FREQUENCY` function and an ***array formula***. To enter the array formula, one selects the entire range in which the frequency distribution will appear, clicks in the Formula Bar window, and then enters the formula, which points to the "data array" (cells A2:A25) and the "bins array" (cells B2:B8). Finally, you press **<Ctrl>** + **<Shift>** + **<Enter>** to place the results of the formula in the output range (see Figure 2-21 for the Formula View revealing the array formula). You cannot enter the array formula separately in each cell, or type the braces around the formula to make it work. It must be entered as described above. Entering an array formula takes both practice and confidence, but it is worth the effort.

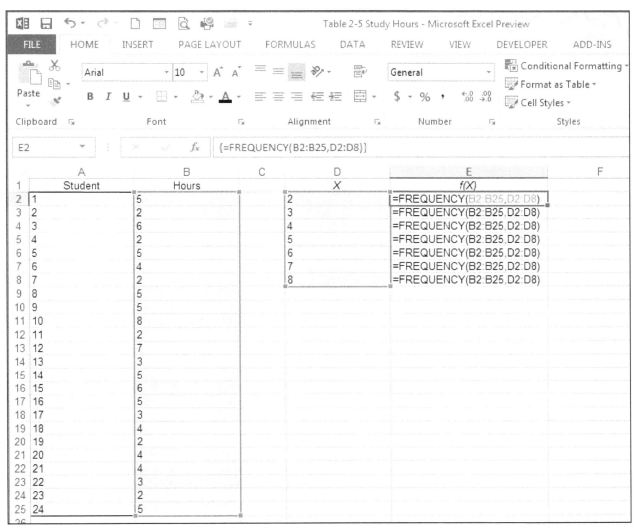

Figure 2-21. Array formula creates a simple frequency distribution

It is also possible to create a simple frequency distribution without the need for array formulas by using the Analysis ToolPak's Histogram tool. To create a frequency table using the Analysis ToolPak, select **Data > Analysis > Data Analysis > Histogram**. Identify the input range and the bins range as before, and the tool will create a simple frequency distribution (see Figure 2-22). The same tool can also be used to produce Pareto charts, cumulative percentage charts, and grouped frequency distributions and histograms. For grouped frequency distributions, the bins are the ***upper limits*** of the class intervals. If you omit the bin range in the Histogram tool's dialog box, Excel will create the bins (or class intervals) automatically.

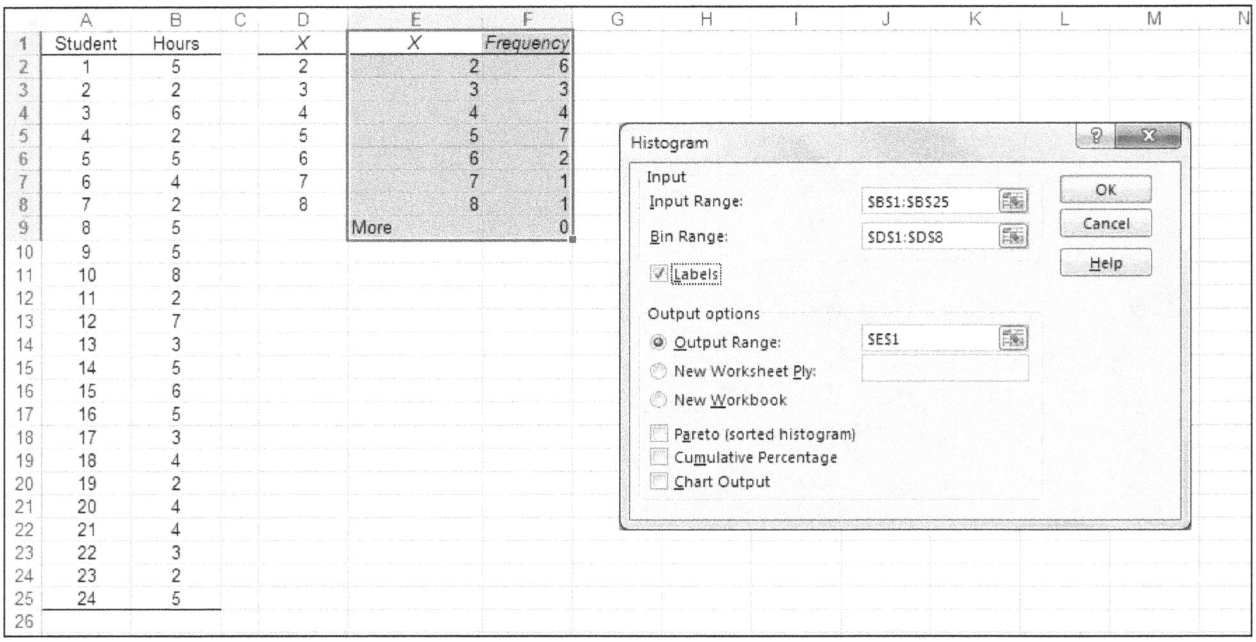

Figure 2-22. Using the Analysis ToolPak to produce a simple frequency distribution

You may specify the bins for grouped frequency distributions by providing a column of the upper limits of the class intervals. For grouped frequency distributions, the results are generally more meaningful when the user supplies the bins instead of allowing Excel to create its own class intervals, as you will see momentarily. There is no exact science to determining the proper number of class intervals, but generally, there should around 10 (Howell, 2008), and certainly no more than 20 intervals (or bins). One rule of thumb for determining the minimum number of class intervals is to find the power to which 2 must be raised to equal or exceed the number of observations in the data set. Another useful rule of thumb for determining the number of class intervals is to find the closest integer to $\sqrt{N}$. Using too few intervals makes the grouped frequency distribution less useful because the patterns or trends in the data are not clearly displayed. Similarly, using too many intervals makes the data appear flatter because most intervals will have few observations (Moore, McCabe, Duckworth, & Sclove, 2003). If you desire greater granularity, and a plot that shows all the data, you might consider producing a dot plot instead of a grouped frequency distribution. MegaStat (See Appendix D) and other Excel statistics add-ins produce dot plots, as do Minitab and other statistics packages.

Return to the data for average wages for the fifty states and Washington D.C. from Table 2-1. For those data, $N = 51$, so that $2^5 = 32 < 51$ or five class intervals would probably be too few intervals, while a minimum of $2^6 = 64 > 51$ or six class intervals should be a good starting point according to one rule of thumb, and $\sqrt{51}=7.1414$ would suggest about seven intervals according to the other rule of thumb. Of course, reason should prevail. Data are often found to have natural breaks and traditional logical intervals. Class intervals of $5,000 make a great deal of sense when dealing with monetary information. Table 2-6 compares the grouped frequency distribution created by Excel (A) with a grouped frequency distribution with manually created bins (B). The data used for the grouped frequency distribution are the 2001 wages for the 50 states and the District of Columbia reported earlier in Table 2-1 (page 56).

Examination of Table 2-6 reveals that Excel may produce class intervals with fractional widths (A), while the user-supplied bin ranges (B) would be obviously more understandable to most users. The frequencies in both the Excel-supplied and the user-supplied bins show the typical positively skewed distribution of income.

Table 2-6. Grouped frequency distributions for data from Table 2-1 with Excel-supplied and user-supplied bins

A. Bins supplied by Excel

Bin	Frequency
25195	1
29582.57143	14
33970.14286	17
38357.71429	11
42745.28571	3
47132.85714	4
51520.42857	0
More	1

B. Bins supplied by user

Bin	Frequency
30000	15
35000	18
40000	12
45000	3
50000	2
55000	0
60000	1

THE BOTTOM LINE
- You can create simple and grouped frequency distributions in Excel with the FREQUENCY function and an array formula.
- For the simple frequency distribution, the "bins" range is the sorted list of possible x values.
- For the grouped frequency distribution, the "bins" range is a column of upper limits for the selected class intervals.
- The number of class intervals for a grouped frequency distribution should be around 10, no more than 20, and somewhere around the square root of the sample size. Reason should prevail when you develop class intervals.
- You can also use the Histogram tool (**Data > Analysis > Data Analysis > Histogram**) to produce simple and grouped frequency distributions.
- If you omit the bins range when using the Histogram tool, Excel will provide its own class intervals.

Finding Percentiles and Percentile Ranks

In addition to simple and grouped frequency distributions, another way to help you determine what a particular raw score means is to transform it to a percentile. A ***percentile*** is the score at or below which a given percent of the cases lie (Welkowitz, Cohen, & Ewen, 2006). To say that a score is at the 5th percentile would indicate that only 5% of the cases were the same or lower, while 95% of the cases were higher than the given raw score. Closely related to the percentile is the ***percentile rank***. This is the percent of cases in the specific reference group (or data set) scoring at or below the given score. Assume that you made a score of 40 on a 50-item test. You could initially take comfort in knowing that you got 80% of the questions right, but you might also be interested in knowing how well you did in comparison to others. Assume the following distribution of 35 scores on the hypothetical test of statistics background knowledge (Table 2-7, and available from the companion web page). Assume your score was 80. What is your percentile rank? The calculations are not particularly difficult, but they can be cumbersome. Excel makes them as simple as using two built-in functions (Figure 2-21).

Table 2-7. Hypothetical test scores for 35 students

Scores	Scores	Scores
52	72	82
59	72	83
62	72	85
67	72	85
67	72	87
67	73	73
67	76	73
67	78	74
69	80	74
69	81	75
70	81	75
70	82	

To find the value associated with a given percentile, one should select a blank cell in the Excel worksheet and enter

$$\text{=PERCENTILE.EXC}(array,\ k)$$

where *array* is the range of cell references or the named range and k is the desired percentile. Oddly, Excel uses values between 0 and 1 for percentiles, so that for the 90th percentile, you would enter 0.90 for k. Let us find the percentiles for increments of 5% for the hypothetical test scores (see columns C and D in the worksheet displayed in Figure 2-19). As it turns out, your raw score of 80 places you somewhere between the 75th and 80th percentiles. To find the percentile rank for a given score, one enters

$$\text{=PERCENTRANK.EXC}(array,\ X,\ [significance])$$

where *array* is the range of cell references or the named range, x is the score being evaluated, and *significance* is an optional argument that specifies the number of significant digits to report. Examine the use of this function in the Formula Bar (see Figure 2-23). If you leave *significance* blank, Excel will report the percentile rank to three digits. To get percentile ranks, it is customary to use the value 2 for significance. Like the PERCENTILE.EXC function, the PERCENTRANK.EXC function reports values between 0 and 1. Your score of 80 has a percentile rank of 75. Seventy-five percent of the class scored the same as or lower than you, and 25% scored higher.

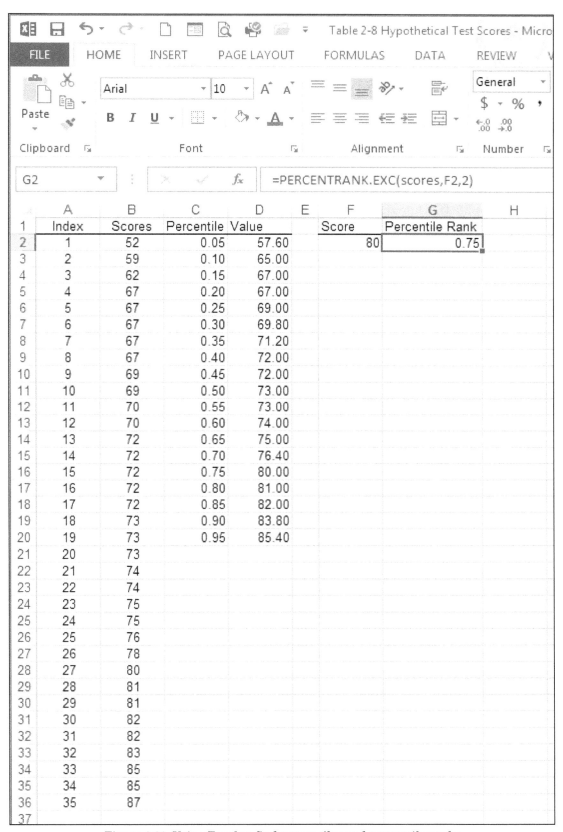

Figure 2-23. Using Excel to find percentiles and percentile ranks

New to Excel—Improved Percentile and Percentile Rank Functions

In Excel 2010 and newer versions, the percentile and percentile rank functions have been improved. Excel now provides the PERCENTILE.EXC, PERCENTILE.INC, PERCENTRANK.EXC, and PERCENTRANK.INC functions. The functions with the *.INC (for *inclusive*) extension will return the same values as the legacy functions from versions 2007 and earlier. The functions with the *.EXC (for *exclusive*) extension will often return a different (and usually more accurate or correct) value, based on the industry standard for that particular function. In Figures 2-24 and 2-25, see the result of using these four functions. The PERCENTILE.EXC function excludes 0 and 1 in the calculation of percentiles (Figure 2-24), while the PERCENTILE.INC function includes both 0 and 1 and produces the same values as the legacy PERCENTILE function.

	B	C	D	E	F	G	H
1							
2	Scores		PERCENTILE.INC	Value		PERCENTILE.EXC	Value
3	52		0.00	52		0.00	#NUM!
4	59		0.05	61		0.05	58
5	62		0.10	67		0.10	65
6	67		0.15	67		0.15	67
7	67		0.20	67		0.20	67
8	67		0.25	69		0.25	69
9	67		0.30	70		0.30	70
10	67		0.35	72		0.35	71
11	69		0.40	72		0.40	72
12	69		0.45	72		0.45	72
13	70		0.50	73		0.50	73
14	70		0.55	73		0.55	73
15	72		0.60	74		0.60	74
16	72		0.65	75		0.65	75
17	72		0.70	76		0.70	76
18	72		0.75	79		0.75	80
19	72		0.80	81		0.80	81
20	73		0.85	82		0.85	82
21	73		0.90	83		0.90	84
22	73		0.95	85		0.95	85
23	74		1.00	87		1.00	#NUM!
24	74						

Figure 2-24. The PERCENTILE.EXC function excludes 0 and 1 from the percentile calculations, and returns some values that are different from those produced by the legacy function

The PERCENTRANK.INC function produces the same value as the legacy PERCENTRANK function, but the PERCENTRANK.EXC function produces a slightly different value (Figure 2-25).

◢	B	C	D	E	F	G
1						
2	Scores		Score	PERCENTRANK.INC	PERCENTRANK.EXC	
3	52		80	0.76	0.75	
4	59					
5	62					
6	67					

Figure 2-25. The two PERCENTRANK functions produce different values

See that the PERCENTILE.EXC function produces the same value for the 75th percentile as does SPSS 20 (Figure 2-26). If you have Excel 2010 or a newer version, you should use the PERCENTILE.EXC and PERCENTRANK.EXC functions. Note that the first quartile is the 25th percentile, and the third quartile is the 75th percentile. Newer versions of Excel also provide the QUARTILE.EXC and QUARTILE.INC functions for finding quartiles, and using the *.EXC functions is compatible with industry standards.

Statistics

Scores

N	Valid	35
	Missing	0
Mean		73.23
Median		73.00
Mode		67[a]
Std. Deviation		7.589
Variance		57.593
Range		35
Minimum		52
Maximum		87
Percentiles	25	69.00
	50	73.00
	75	80.00

a. Multiple modes exist. The smallest value is shown

Figure 2-26. PERCENTILE.EXC function returns the same value for the 75th percentile as SPSS

THE BOTTOM LINE
- The value associated with a particular **percentile** such as the 5th percentile, is the score at or below which a given percent of the distribution falls, in this case 61.1. The 5th percentile score is 61.1.
- A **percentile rank** gives the percentage of scores, for example 25%, that lie at or below a given score, in this case 69. The percentile rank of 69 is 25.
- Excel implements these functions as PERCENTILE.EXC(array,k) where *array* is the data, and *k* is the desired percentile, and PERCENTRANK.EXC(array,X,[significance]) where *array* is the

data, *x* is the score being evaluated, and significance is an optional argument specifying the number of significant digits in the percentile rank for *x*.
- The functions with an *.INC (for inclusive) extension are for compatibility with the earlier versions of Excel, while the *.EXC (for exclusive) functions are compatible with industry standards.

Chapter 2 Exercises

1. Open the worksheet for Table 2-7 and use the Analysis ToolPak's Descriptive Statistics tool to find the mean, mode, median, count, minimum, maximum, range, variance, and standard deviation for the 35 hypothetical test scores.

2. Using the same workbook file, use Excel's built-in functions to compare the values of the standard deviation and variance treating the data set as a sample and treating the data set as a population.

3. Open the workbook file for Table 2-1 and use the Analysis ToolPak's Descriptive Statistics tool to calculate the mean, mode, median, count, minimum, maximum, range, variance, and standard deviation of the *PctChg* variable for the 51 records. What does the average percent change tell you about the wage level differences between 2001 and 2002?

4. Using the same data set, find the percentile ranks for 2002 wages for the District of Columbia and your own state of residence. What is the 90th percentile for 2002 wages? What is the 10th percentile?

3 Charts, Graphs, and More Tables

In Chapter 3, you learn how to create charts and graphs and use the PivotTable tool. Charts and graphs are easily constructed and modified in Excel, and can be displayed alongside the data for ease of visualization. The charts and graphs are dynamically linked to the data, and update automatically when the data are modified. This chapter covers the following:

- Pie charts
- Bar charts
- Histograms
- Line graphs
- Scatterplots
- Pivot tables

Excel provides options for adding three-dimensional effects and other creative formatting to your charts and graphs. For statistics, you should be careful not to overuse these embellishments. For example, using 3-D column charts and pie charts distorts the data and introduces a false third dimension. Simpler is definitely better here. For a discussion of common graphical distortions and some good recommendations for avoiding them, see Bennett, Briggs, and Triola (2009).

Pie Charts

A pie chart divides a circle into relatively larger and smaller slices based on the relative frequencies or percentages of observations in different categories. The following data (see Table 3-1) are summarized from the data set introduced in Chapter 2, the 2001 and 2002 wages for covered employees in the 50 states and the District of Columbia. The PivotTable tool discussed later in this chapter was used to count the number of states in each region.

Table 3-1. Data for pie and bar charts

Region	Count
Midwest	12
Northeast	9
South	17
West	13

To construct a pie chart in Excel 2010, select the data including the labels and then click **Insert > Charts > Pie.** Choose the plain 2-D pie chart. See the completed pie chart in Figure 3-1. Charts are graphic objects that are not attached to a cell or cells in the workbook. The chart object is also named and is available from the Name Manager and the Name Box. You can move, copy, resize, and delete chart objects quite easily. It is also simple to copy the object and paste charts into Microsoft Word or PowerPoint for reports and presentations. Excel provides full-color formatting for these graphic objects.

When you create a chart or graph, you will have access to a **Chart Tools** group with ribbon tabs for **Design**, **Layout**, and **Format**. Excel comes with a gallery of chart styles on the **Design** ribbon (**Chart Tools > Design > Chart Styles**), and the **Layout** and **Format** ribbons provide options for customizing chart objects (see Figure 3-2). Note you can also summarize the data with a pivot table and produce various charts from the pivot table. We will discuss the pivot table in more detail later in this chapter.

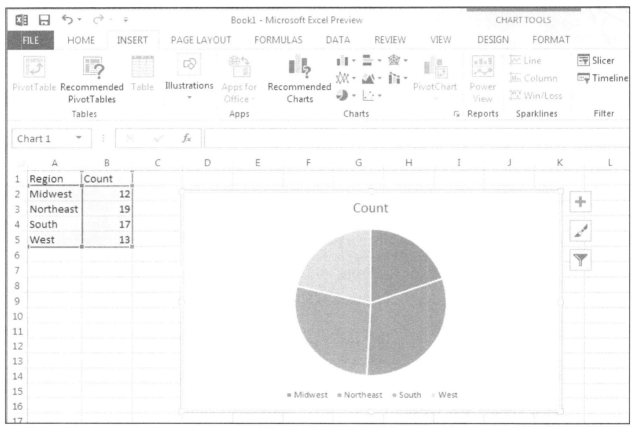

Figure 3-1. Pie chart

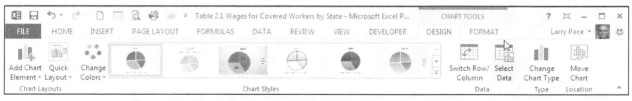

Figure 3-2. Chart Tools menu adds Design, Layout and Format tabs

Bar Charts

Use the same data to produce a bar chart. Although Excel has a chart type labeled "bar," it is horizontal in orientation and should be avoided. To generate a bar chart in Excel, follow the steps for the pie chart above, but select **Column** as the chart type. You may modify the bar chart by varying the colors, patterns, or grayscale shades of the bars. To do so, right-click on one of the bars and then select **Format Data Series**. Select the option "**Vary colors by point**" under the **Fill** menu (see Figure 3-3 for the result).

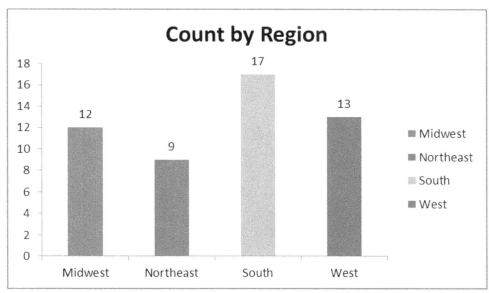

Figure 3-3. Bar chart using different colors for separate bars

Histograms

The x axis in a histogram represents a continuum of quantitative values, so the bars should touch. The study hour data used to produce a frequency distribution in Chapter 2 (see Table 2-5, page 66) are used to illustrate the histogram. Produce the histogram using the **Column** option in the **Charts** group (**Insert > Charts > Column**), but select only the array of frequencies. Do not include the "bins" (the x values) in the adjacent column. These will be used as category labels for the x axis. Excel by default will label the columns beginning with 1. Sometimes this is appropriate, but usually it is not. You can pick any axis labels—numerical or text—that you would like for your histogram or other chart object.

After selecting the frequencies as your source data and producing your initial histogram, click the **Select Data** icon in the **Design** ribbon and enter the cell references to the bins as your Category (X) axis labels (see Figure 3-4). Remember that to reach the **Design** ribbon, you must select the histogram or click on its name in the Name Box. It is also easy to click on the default axis labels and then right-click to select the data. When you select the chart or click in it, its default name will appear in the Name Box and the **Chart Tools** options will reappear.

To remove the unwanted gaps between the bars of your histogram, right-click on one of the bars and select **Format Data Series** (Figure 3-4). Change the gap size to zero under **Series Options**. The completed histogram is displayed in Figure 3-5. As with all charts and graphs, you can use a gallery style or you can customize your histogram with a title and axis labels from the **Layout** ribbon under **Chart Tools**.

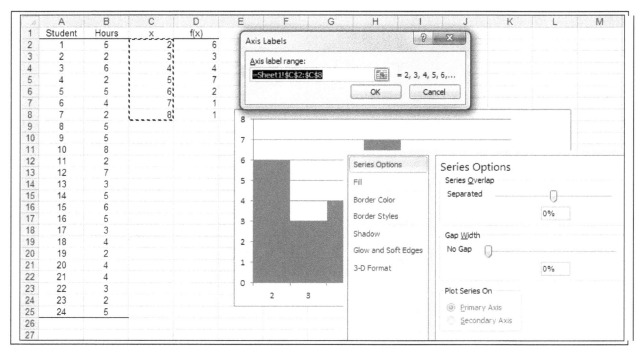

Figure 3-4. Adding *X*-axis category labels and removing gaps

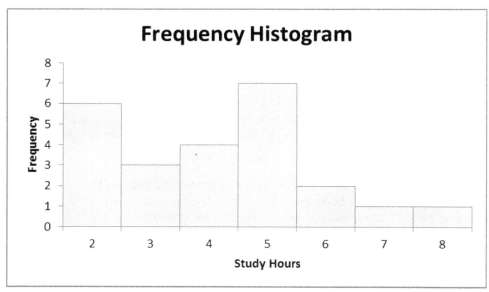

Figure 3-5. Completed frequency histogram with gaps removed and title and axis labels added

Line Graphs

A frequency polygon is a special kind of line graph. We use the data from the previous section to illustrate. Select **Insert > Charts > Line** as shown in Figure 3-6. Once again, select only the frequencies, not the *x* values. Select "Line with Markers" in the 2-D line graph menu. If you do happen to select the *x* values along with the frequencies, Excel will make a graph with two lines (voice of experience again). Add the correct *x* axis category labels as with the histogram. In Excel 2013, the icons next to the frequency polygon provide formatting options such as axis titles and a style gallery options. The completed frequency polygon using one of the predefined styles appears in Figure 3-7. This particular style provides the frequency value in a circle for each value of x.

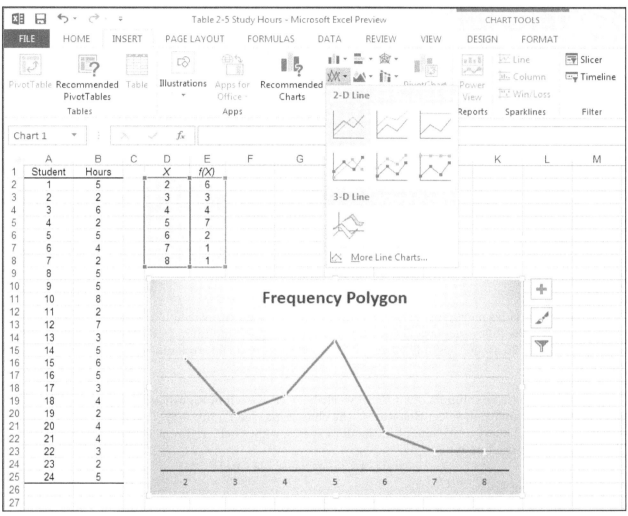

Figure 3-6. Producing a line graph in Excel

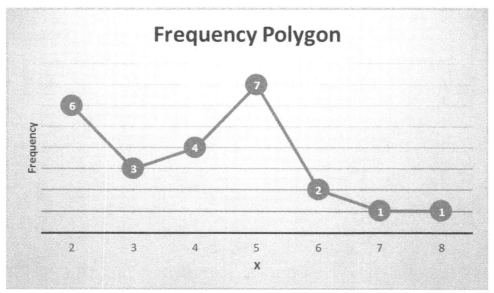

Figure 3-7. Completed frequency polygon

Scatterplots

A scatterplot provides a graphical view of pairs of measures on two variables, x and y. Assume that you were given the following data (Table 3-2, available at the companion web page) concerning the number of hours 20 students study each week (on average) and the students' GPA (grade point average).

Place the data in three columns of an Excel worksheet, as shown in Figure 3-8. As before, select **Insert**, **Charts**, and then select **Scatter** as the chart type (see Figure 3-8). To add the trend line (see Figure 3-9), left-click on any element in the data series, right-click, and select **Add Trendline**. Select **Linear** as the line type.

Table 3-2. Study hours and GPA

Student	Hours	GPA	Student	Hours	GPA
1	10	3.33	11	13	3.26
2	12	2.92	12	12	3.00
3	10	2.56	13	11	2.74
4	15	3.08	14	10	2.85
5	14	3.57	15	13	3.33
6	12	3.31	16	13	3.29
7	13	3.45	17	14	3.58
8	15	3.93	18	18	3.85
9	16	3.82	19	17	4.00
10	14	3.70	20	14	3.50

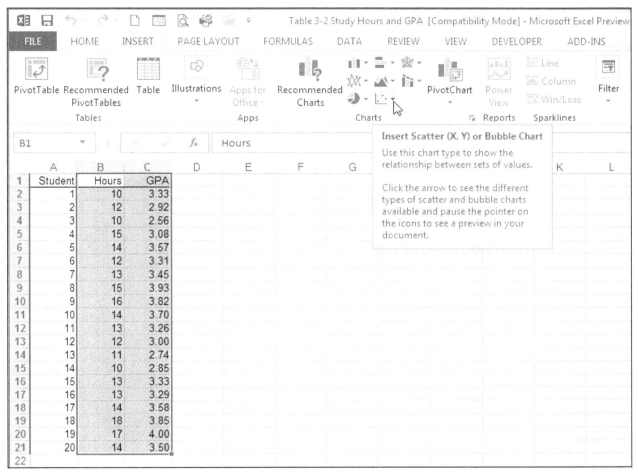

Figure 3-8. Generating a scatterplot in Excel

The scatterplot appears in Figure 3-9. As with the other graphics, I added axis titles and removed the grid lines.

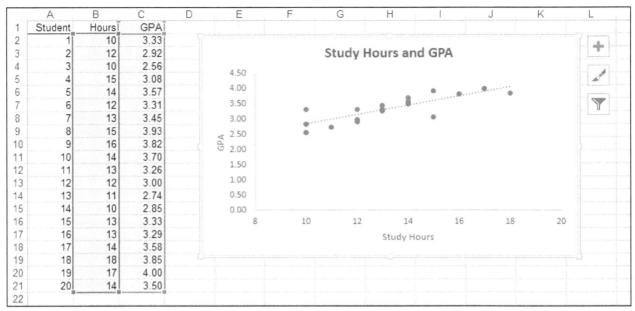

Figure 3-9. Completed scatterplot

THE BOTTOM LINE

- To insert a pie chart, bar chart, line chart, scatterplot, or other chart in Excel, select the relevant data then **Insert > Charts** and then select the desired chart and options.
- For line graphs and histograms, the x axis labels should be added after the chart is created.
- Charts are not attached to specific cells in the worksheet.
- Charts can be moved, sized, formatted, copied, and deleted.
- When you create a chart in Excel, it is dynamically linked to the data.
- Charts are special named objects and as such are available via the Name Box and the Name Manager.
- When you create a chart, you have access to **Chart Tools** with **Design**, **Format**, and **Layout** ribbons.

Pivot Tables

Forty college students who like peanut M&Ms and expressed a color preference provided the responses in Table 3-3. To use the pivot table features of Excel, you must first place the data in a single column of an Excel worksheet, as shown in Figure 3-10. It this case it is very important to have a column heading. Otherwise, the pivot table tool will take the first entry as the label and reduce the number of observations by one. You could use the label "Color" for the column heading.

Table 3-3. Peanut M&M color preferences for 40 college students

Preference	Preference	Preference	Preference
Green	Blue	Red	Red
Blue	Green	Red	Green
Green	Brown	Green	Blue
Green	Green	Red	Blue
Red	Red	Yellow	Red
Green	Blue	Blue	Green
Blue	Blue	Blue	Blue
Blue	Brown	Blue	Blue
Yellow	Brown	Orange	Red
Green	Yellow	Blue	Orange

	A	B	C
1	Color		
2	Green		
3	Blue		
4	Green		
5	Green		
6	Red		
7	Green		
8	Blue		
9	Blue		

Figure 3-10. M&M color preferences of 40 college students (partial data)

The pivot table tool makes it possible to count and summarize text entries as well as numerical values. As with other graphic objects, you can choose from a gallery of predefined styles for your pivot table. This tool can also summarize quantitative data, as we will discuss shortly

To create the pivot table, select the entire data range including the column heading and then select **Insert > Tables > PivotTable** (see Figure 3-11). You will see a dialog box with the data highlighted. Accept the defaults and click **OK** to launch the PivotTable Tools. If your data are formatted as a table, you can also select **Table Tools > Design > Tools > Summarize with PivotTable**.

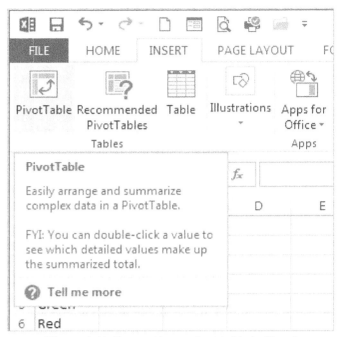

Figure 3-11. Generating a pivot table in Excel

In the dialog box (see Figure 3-12), select the data range and click **OK**. It is usually best to put the pivot table in a new worksheet.

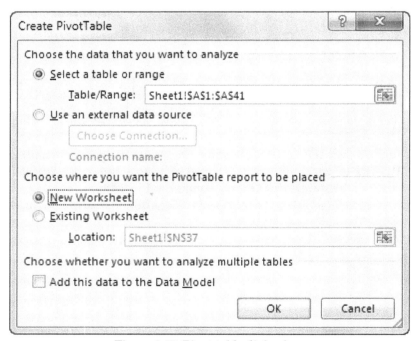

Figure 3-12. Pivot table dialog box

You will now see a **PivotTable Tools** menu with an **Options** ribbon and a **Design** ribbon. In the PivotTable Field List, click and drag the "Color" item to the Row Labels area, and then drag the "Color" item to the Values area (see Figure 3-13). Because the data are text entries, Excel will alphabetize the labels for lack of any other organizing principle. You can sort the data by count if you choose. In my personal experience, it is often better to copy the pivot table and paste it to a new location in the workbook if you want to manipulate the data further or produce graphics like pie or bar charts.

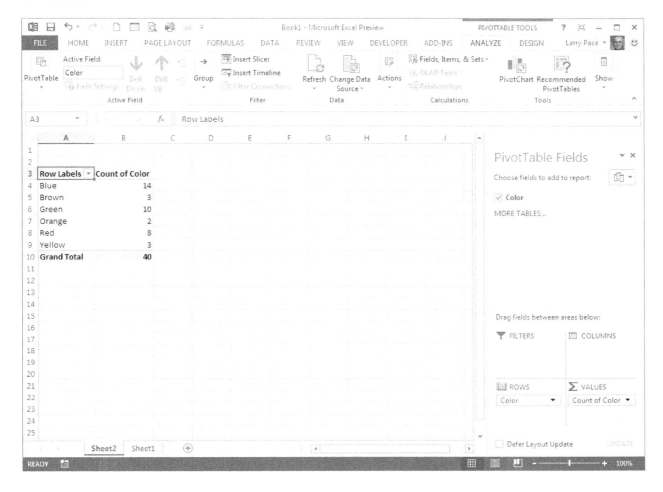

Figure 3-13. Pivot table in a new worksheet

The completed pivot table, after application of the default table formatting, appears in Table 3-4.

Table 3-4. Completed pivot table

Color	Preference
Blue	14
Green	10
Red	8
Yellow	3
Brown	3
Orange	2

In addition to one-way tables, you can use the Pivot Table tool to create two-way contingency tables. Drag one variable to the row area and the other to the column area to create a cross-tabulation.

When data being entered into a pivot table are numerical rather than text labels, Excel will sum these numbers by default. You can change the field settings in the pivot table to count or average the values. In the **PivotTable Tools > Options** ribbon, click on **Field Settings** in the **Active Field** group to change these settings. (see Figure 3-13).

THE BOTTOM LINE
- Pivot tables can summarize both numerical and text entries for one or two variables (categories).
- To create a pivot table, select the relevant data and then select **Insert > Tables > PivotTable**.
- Creating a pivot table gives access to a **PivotTable Tools** group with **Options** and **Design** ribbons.

Using the Pivot Table Tool to Summarize Quantitative Data

The following hypothetical data represent the sex, industry, age, and salary in thousands of dollars for 50 CEOs (see Table 3-5). You can use a pivot table to summarize the CEOs' ages by sex and industry.

Table 3-5. Hypothetical CEO data

Sex	Industry	Age	Salary	Sex	Industry	Age	Salary
1	1	53	145	0	2	51	368
1	2	33	262	0	1	48	659
1	3	45	208	0	2	45	396
1	3	36	192	0	2	37	300
1	2	62	324	0	1	50	343
1	3	58	214	0	2	50	536
1	2	61	254	0	2	50	543
1	3	56	205	0	1	53	298
1	2	44	203	0	2	70	1103
1	3	46	250	0	1	53	406
1	3	63	149	0	2	47	862
1	3	70	213	0	1	48	298
1	1	44	155	0	1	38	350
1	3	50	200	0	3	74	800
1	1	52	250	0	1	60	726
0	1	43	324	0	3	32	370
0	1	46	362	0	1	51	536
0	2	55	424	0	3	50	291
0	1	41	294	0	1	40	808
0	1	55	632	0	3	61	543
0	2	55	498	0	3	56	350
0	1	50	369	0	1	45	242
0	2	49	390	0	3	61	467
0	2	47	332	0	2	59	317
0	1	69	750	0	3	57	317

The data should be placed in four columns in an Excel worksheet (see Figure 3-14). For illustrative purposes, assume that sex is coded 1 (*male*) and 0 (*female*), and that the industries are 1 (*manufacturing*), 2 (*retail*), and 3 (*service*). Use sex as the column field and industry as the row field. Then find the averages of the salaries for male and female CEOs in each industry.

	A	B	C	D
1	Sex	Industry	Age	Salary
2	1	1	53	145
3	1	2	33	262
4	1	3	45	208
5	1	3	36	192
6	1	2	62	324
7	1	3	58	214
8	1	2	61	254
9	1	3	56	205
10	1	2	44	203
11	1	3	46	250
42	0	3	32	370
43	0	1	51	636
44	0	3	50	291
45	0	1	40	808

Figure 3-14. CEO Data in Excel worksheet (partial data)

To build the pivot table, select the entire data set including the row of column headings, and then click on **Insert > Tables > PivotTable**. Accept the defaults to place the pivot table in a new worksheet (see Figure 3-15). In the PivotTable Field List, drag the "sex" item to the columns field and the "industry" item to the rows field as shown in Figure 3-16. You can then move the salary field to the Values area and change the field settings to Average, as shown in Figure 3-17.

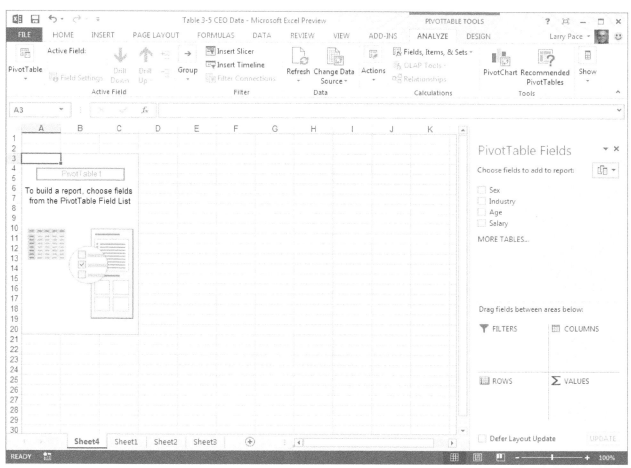

Figure 3-15. Preparation for the pivot table

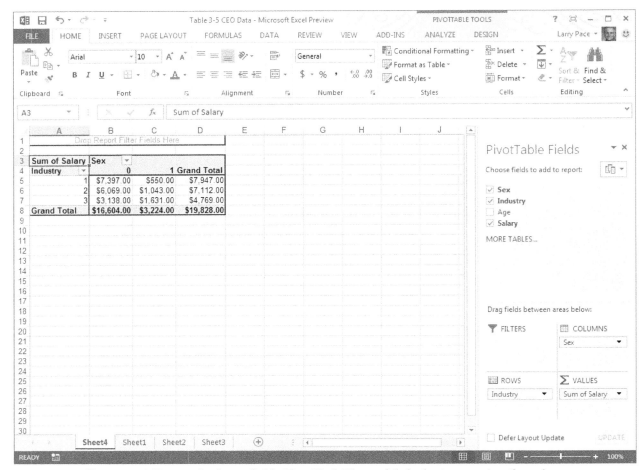

Figure 3-16. Row and column fields identified. The tool defaults to summing the values

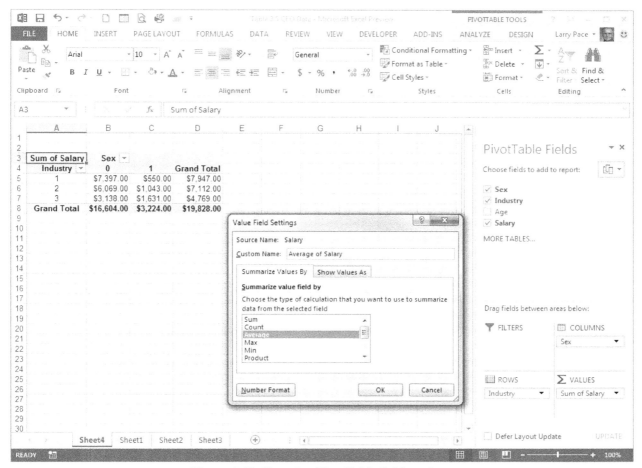

Figure 3-17. Changing PivotTable field settings

The finished pivot table after some number formatting appears in Figure 3-18. I often use the Pivot Table tool to summarize quantitative data, but usually copy the information to a new location in the workbook so that I can manipulate it more easily outside the pivot table framework.

Average of Salary	Sex		
Industry	0	1	Grand Total
1	$462.31	$183.33	$418.26
2	$505.75	$260.75	$444.50
3	$448.29	$203.88	$317.93
Grand Total	$474.40	$214.93	$396.56

Figure 3-18. Finished pivot table

Your table may not have the same labels as the one shown in Figure 3-18. To see the various formatting options, you can select **PIVOTTABLE TOOLS > PivotTable > Options (**see Figure 3-19). More directly, you can right click directly in the pivot table to get options dialog.

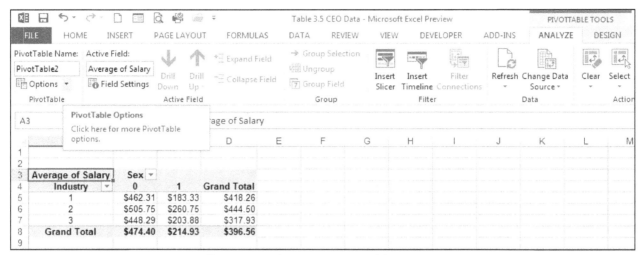

Figure 3-19. Accessing pivot table options

THE BOTTOM LINE

- The pivot table tool can be used to summarize a quantitative variable for different levels of one or two categorical variables.
- The row, column, and values to be summarized are entered through the PivotTable Field List.
- The default field setting for quantitative variables is the sum.
- Variable settings can be changed to summarize by count, average, or other statistics.

Additional Charts Excel Does Not Do Easily

There are many charts and plots commonly used in exploratory data analysis (Tukey, 1977) including boxplots, dot plots, and stem-and-leaf plots. Dedicated statistics packages such as Minitab and SPSS provide these additional charts and plots. However, Excel does not produce these charts and plots easily. You can make a boxplot or a dotplot with a little manipulation of the Chart Wizard, by use of a third-party add-in, or with macros. A cursory Internet search will reveal that there are workarounds available to construct these "missing" charts and graphs in Excel.

As mentioned, third-party add-ins provide Excel with many of these missing graphical tools, along with enhanced statistical capabilities. In my opinion, the most effective add-in is MegaStat, which is distributed by McGraw-Hill. Other available statistics add-ins are PHStat from Pearson Prentice Hall, Data Desk/XL, and the Analysis ToolPak Plus from Cengage. Below is a boxplot of the ages of the 50 CEOs shown in Table 3-5. This boxplot was produced in MegaStat (see Figure 3-20). A brief appendix (Appendix D) shows how to get and use MegaStat.

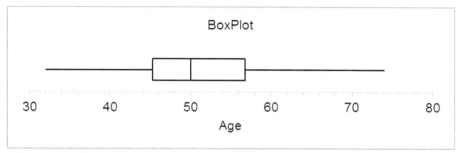

Figure 3-20. Boxplot provides a graphical display of the five-number summary

As another example of a useful plot in MegaStat that Excel's Chart Wizard does not provide, examine the dot plot for the body temperatures of 130 adults (see Chapter 5 for details on this data set). The dot plot is similar to a histogram, but has the advantage of "granularity," as every data point is represented (see Figure 3-20).

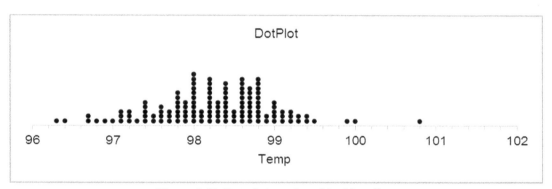

Figure 3-21. Dot plot produced by MegaStat

THE BOTTOM LINE
- Excel does not have built-in dot plots, boxplots, or stem-and-leaf plots.
- Statistical packages and Excel add-ins provide these "missing" plots.
- Manipulation of the Chart tool can also produce some of these missing features.

Chapter 3 Exercises

1. Use the pivot table tool to summarize the average 2002 wages for covered workers for each region (see Table 2-1).

2. Use the information you just generated to make a bar chart of the average wages by region.

3. Make a side-by-side (clustered) bar chart showing the 2001 and 2002 wages by region.

4. Summarize the average percent change in wages by region.

5. The following data were obtained from the Bureau of Labor Statistics, Current Population Survey. The data represent 2007 unemployment in percentage and 2007 weekly wages in dollars for people with various education levels. Enter the data in an Excel workbook file (or retrieve the file from the course data sets). Produce a bar chart to show the percentage of unemployment by educational attainment.

Education	Unemployment	WeeklyWage
No high-school diploma	7.1	428
High-school graduate	4.4	604
Some college, no degree	3.8	683
Associate degree	3.0	740
Bachelor's degree	2.2	987
Master's degree	1.8	1165
Professional Degree	1.3	1427
Doctoral Degree	1.4	1497

6. Using the same data as above, produce a bar chart to show the average weekly wages by educational attainment.

7. Using the data in Table 3-5, produce a scatterplot of the relationship between age and salary. Produce separate scatterplots for male and female CEOs.

4 Working with z Scores and the Standard Normal Distribution

In this chapter, you will learn how to use the STANDARDIZE function in Excel to produce z scores from raw data. You will review Chebyshev's Inequality and the Empirical Rule. You will learn how to use the NORM.S.DIST and NORM.S.INV functions and simple formulas to find areas to the left and right of given z scores in the standard normal distribution, the area between two z scores, the probability of a given z score, and the z score for a given probability. Finally, you will learn how to use the data filtering options of Excel to compare theoretical and empirical probabilities.

What is a z Score?

A z score is a "combination" statistic that shows how far away from the mean of the distribution any particular raw score is, both in direction (the sign shows whether the raw score is higher than or lower than the mean) and in magnitude.

For a population, the z score for any raw score is the deviation score (the difference between the raw score and the population mean) divided by the population standard deviation:

$$z = \frac{x - \mu_x}{\sigma_x}$$

For sample data you can calculate a z score for any raw score x by using the following formula. We simply replace the population mean with the sample mean and the population standard deviation with the sample standard deviation.

$$z = \frac{x - \overline{x}}{s_x}$$

Recall the example from Chapter 2 used to illustrate percentiles for a hypothetical set of scores (see Table 2-7, page 59). You scored 80 on the test. Your percentile rank was 76 (or 75 if you used PERCENTRANK.EXC). You could also calculate your z score. To do that, you would need the mean (73.32) and the standard deviation (7.59), which you can find using the Descriptive Statistics tool or the AVERAGE and STDEV functions. To calculate your z score, subtract the mean from that score, and divide the resulting difference by the standard deviation. Your z score is .89. Although the computations for a z score are simple, Excel provides a function called STANDARDIZE that will return the z score for a given value of x, the mean, and the standard deviation of the data set or the population. To find your z score, you could simply type the following into the blank cell where you want the z score to appear, and then press **<Enter>**.

```
=STANDARDIZE(80, 73.32, 7.59)
```

The value of z shows how many standard deviation units away from the mean the raw score is. A z score of -3 indicates that the raw score is 3 standard deviations below the mean. A z score of $+2.47$

indicates that the raw score is 2.47 standard deviations above the mean. Thus, your *z* score on the hypothetical test means that you scored .89 standard deviations above the mean. As with a percentile rank, you can use the *z* score as an indicator of the relative location of a given raw score in the distribution.

When the data are approximately normally distributed, you can use the standard normal distribution to approximate percentile ranks. Using the previous example, determine what your percentile rank would be given that the hypothetical test scores were normally distributed. To do that, use the NORM.S.DSIST function to evaluate your *z* score. Enter a blank worksheet cell and type

```
=NORM.S.DIST(0.89, TRUE)
```

The resulting value, .81 (or the 81st percentile), is close to the 75th percentile you found earlier. In the standard normal distribution, 81 percent of the values are equal to or below .89 standard deviations above the mean.

New to Excel

As you see from the above, Excel 2010, 2011, and 2013 have the NORM.S.DIST function. This function has the following form:

```
=NORM.S.DIST(z, CUMULATIVE)
```

The value of CUMULATIVE is either TRUE (for the cumulative standard normal distribution) or FALSE (for the standard normal probability density function). The cumulative standard normal distribution shows the area to the left of a given *z* score. By changing its statistical functions to this form, Microsoft has taken a big step toward making Excel a better (and more standardized) statistical package.

Chebyshev's Inequality and the Empirical Rule

The *z* scores for any sample of data, whether the data are normally distributed or not, will by definition have a mean of 0 and a standard deviation of 1. Although a mean of zero is important in standardized scores, it has no relationship to the zero used in a ratio scale of measurement to represent the absence of the quantity being measured (Roscoe, 1975). As the sample becomes more normally distributed, the standard normal distribution becomes increasingly helpful in making decisions about probabilities. Standard scores are useful even when data are not normally distributed, because they help us know how extreme a particular score is in any distribution.

Chebyshev's Inequality states that in a distribution of any shape, no more than $1/k^2$ of the values will be more than k standard deviations away from the mean for any value of k greater than 1. Thus, no more than 1/4 of the values will be more than ±2 standard deviations away from the mean. Said differently, at least 3/4 or 75% of the values will be within ±2 standard deviations of the mean in any distribution. No more than 1/9 of the values will be more than ±3 standard deviations away from the mean. Said differently, at least 8/9 or 89% of the values will be within ±3 standard deviations of the mean.

When the distribution of values is "mound-shaped" and symmetrical like the normal distribution, with most of the values close to the mean and with the relative frequencies tapering off in the tails of the distribution, you can apply the tighter standards of the *Empirical Rule*:

- ☐ Approximately 68.3% of the values will be within ±1 standard deviation of the mean
- ☐ Approximately 95.4% of the values will be within ±2 standard deviations of the mean
- ☐ A vast majority (about 99.7%) of the values will be within ±3 standard deviations of the mean

Use the NORM.S.INV Function for Critical Values

Excel makes it easy to find the probabilities associated with intervals under the standard normal curve, and thus eliminates the need for tabled values of the standard normal distribution. The built-in functions NORM.S.DIST and NORM.S.INV make it possible to "look up" a probability for any z score or to look up a z score (or scores) for any given probability.

For the standard normal distribution, Excel provides a function called NORM.S.INV that can be used to find even more precise limits than those stated by the Empirical Rule. This function makes the use of tables of the standard normal distribution unnecessary. The critical values of z for a 95% confidence interval are $z = \pm 1.960$. If you are using an earlier version of Excel, use the NORMSINV function to find these values. Because the standard normal distribution is symmetrical, if you find a value of z that separates the upper 2.5% of the standard normal distribution from the lower 97.5%, the same value with a negative sign will separate the lower 2.5% from the upper 97.5%, leaving the desired 95% in the middle. Thus, the area beyond (to the right) of the upper critical value and the area beyond (to the left) of the lower critical value in this instance will add up to 5%, and the area between these two critical values will be 95%. To find these critical values in Excel, you can simply type the following into a blank worksheet cell where you want the result to display

```
=NORM.S.INV(.975)
```

and Excel will return the value 1.959963985 ≈ 1.960. You can also type in

```
=NORM.S.INV(.025)
```

and receive the result −1.959963985 ≈ −1.960. Because the normal distribution is symmetrical, these two values will always be the same numerical value, differing only in sign. We often abbreviate the critical values as $z = \pm 1.960$. By understanding the symmetry, when you have found one critical value, you have automatically found the other. If you are using a previous version of Excel, the legacy function is:

```
=NORMSINV(p)
```

The Standard Normal Distribution

When a normal distribution is converted to z scores, you obtain the standard normal distribution. Any normal random variable x with a mean of μ and a standard deviation of σ can be converted to the standard normal distribution by a simple transformation:

$$z = \frac{x - \mu}{\sigma}$$

The inverse transformation of z to x is also made possible by use of a little algebra:

$$x = \mu + z\sigma$$

When the population parameters are unknown, use sample statistics to calculate z:

$$z = \frac{x - \bar{x}}{s}$$

and

$$x = \bar{x} + zs$$

As you have already seen, Excel provides a number of functions for working with standard (z) scores and the normal distribution. Because there are infinitely many possible normal distributions, it is most convenient to work with the standard normal distribution (see Figure 4-1).

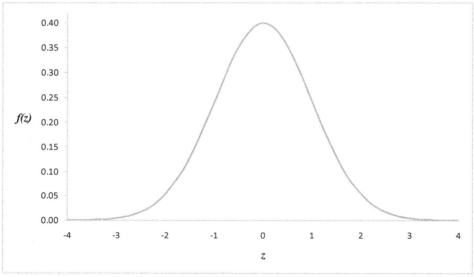

Figure 4-1. The standard normal curve

THE BOTTOM LINE

- A z score is a combination statistic showing how many standard deviation units away from the mean a given raw score is, and in which direction (above or below the mean).
- By definition, z scores for any data set will have a mean of 0 and a standard deviation of 1.
- The limits of Chebyshev's Inequality tell us what percentage of scores will fall within a certain number of standard deviation units from the mean is in a distribution of any shape.
- When data are normally distributed, we can use the Empirical Rule to determine what percentage of scores will lie a certain number of standard deviation units from the mean.
- Excel provides the STANDARDIZE function to calculate z scores.
- Excel provides the NORM.S.DIST function to find the probability of a given z score in the standard normal distribution.
- Excel provides the NORM.S.INV function to find the z score associated with a given probability.

Finding Areas under the Standard Normal Curve

You are most often interested in finding the areas for four kinds of intervals in the standard normal distribution (see Figure 4-2):

☐ the area to the left of a given z score, a *left-tailed* probability,
☐ the area to the right of a given z score, a *right-tailed* probability,
☐ the area between two given z scores, an interval with upper and lower limits, and
☐ the combined area to the left of one z score and the right of another z score, usually the same z score in absolute value and differing only in sign, (a *two-tailed* probability).

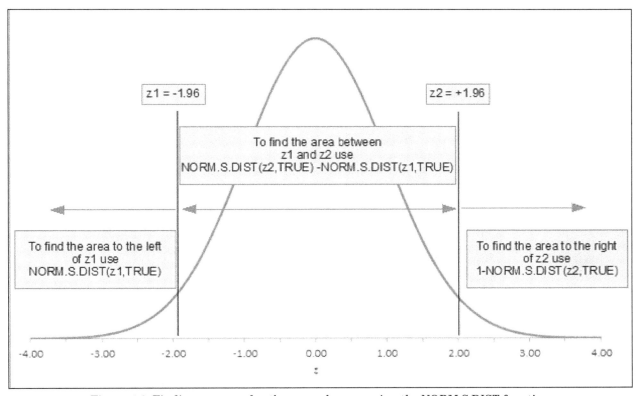

Figure 4-2. Finding areas under the normal curve using the NORM.S.DIST function

The normal distribution theoretically ranges from $-\infty$ to $+\infty$, and the curve never touches the x axis. Technically, a left-tailed probability has the limits $-\infty$ and z, and a right-tailed probability has the limits z and $+\infty$. However, the majority of the area of the standard normal curve lies between ±3 standard deviations, and statistics textbooks rarely have tables that exceed values of $z = ±4$. As you have seen, Excel 2010 provides a function called NORM.S.DIST(z,CUMULATIVE). Use of this function allows one to find any area to the left of a given z score in the standard normal distribution. In addition, as discussed above, Excel also provides the NORMS.INV(p) function for finding the value(s) of z associated with a given probability.

In addition to its functions for the standard normal distribution, Excel also provides a function labeled NORM.DIST (without the first "S") for normal distributions with any mean and standard deviation, and the inverse of this function, NORM.INV, for finding the area associated with a given raw score. However, it is simpler and less confusing to convert raw data to standard scores and use the standard normal distribution. The NORM.DIST function requires four arguments (*x*, the mean, the standard deviation, and CUMULATIVE) and the NORM.INV function requires three arguments (the probability, the mean, and the standard deviation).

Calculating *z* Scores with the STANDARDIZE Function

Let us return to the CEO data from Chapter 3 (Table 3-5, page 77) and find the *z* scores for the ages of the CEOs. To clarify matters, you can name the range of 50 ages, and then use this name in functions and formulas. See the new column called *zAge* for the *z* scores (see Figure 4-3). Observe in cell E2 the *z* score for the first age in cell C2, and the use of the STANDARDIZE function in the Formula Bar.

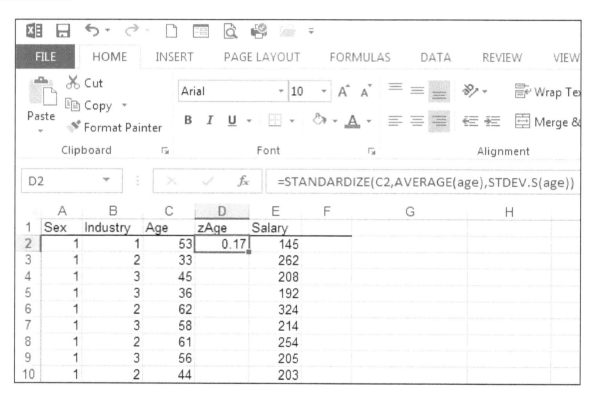

Figure 4-3. Using the STANDARDIZE function to find a *z* score

As you saw at the beginning of the chapter, the STANDARDIZE function requires as its three arguments the particular value of *x* being evaluated, the mean of *x*, and the standard deviation of *x*. We used the device of including the AVERAGE and STDEV.S functions within the STANDARDIZE function. By using a relative reference to cell C2 in the formula in cell E2 (look again in the Formula Bar in Figure 4-3 to see the function), you can now copy that formula from cell E2 to the other cells in column E. The named range uses absolute cell references, so the formula will increment correctly, and all the *z* scores will be computed correctly when the formula is pasted to the remainder of the range in column E (see Figure 4-4).

The average *z* score is zero, and the standard deviation of the *z* scores is 1 by definition (see Figure 4-4). You should be aware that Excel accumulates and reports rounding error, so that the original average reported in cell E52 (see Figure 4-4) was shown in scientific notation as −2.53131E−16. This general number formatting throws off many students, but one should realize that this number is essentially zero. It is a decimal followed by fifteen zeros and then 253131. To see the result in a more expected and reassuring format, select the cell, then click on the Launch Number Format dialog icon in the **Number** group of the **Home** ribbon (or simply right-click to get the **Format Cells** option) and change the cell's number format to, say, four decimal places.

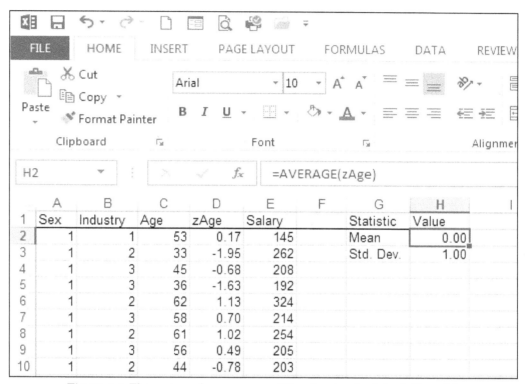

Figure 4-4. The z scores have a mean of 0 and a standard deviation of 1.

As discussed earlier, finding the area to the left of a z score, the area to the right of a z score, and the areas either between or beyond two z scores are common problems in statistics. Excel makes finding such areas easy, and makes the use of statistical tables unnecessary, as demonstrated below.

Finding the Area to the Left of a z Score

Assume that the prices of homes in a given area (perhaps the Kansas City area) are normally distributed with a mean of $220,000 and a standard deviation of $50,000. What is the probability that a randomly selected house in this area will have a price less than $150,000? First, calculate a z score, and then find the area to the left of that z score because we are interested in a left-tailed ("less than") probability. For convenience, express all the variables in thousands of dollars:

$$z = \frac{x - \bar{x}}{s} = \frac{150 - 220}{50} = -1.40$$

You can find this value in Excel by typing

```
=STANDARDIZE(150,220,50)
```

into a blank cell of the worksheet and pressing **<Enter>**. As you have seen, the three arguments for the STANDARDIZE function are, in order, the value of x being evaluated, the value of the population or sample mean, and the value of the population or sample standard deviation.

Examine the table of the standard normal distribution in the back of virtually any statistics text and find that the area to the left of a z score of the value −1.4 is approximately .0808. You can use the NORM.S.DIST(z) function in Excel to find that the probability is, more precisely, 0.080756659. To find this value in Excel, type:

```
=NORM.S.DIST(-1.4, TRUE)
```

Remember, the first argument for the NORMSDIST function is the value of z or a pointer to the cell containing the value. The second argument is a logical TRUE for the cumulative probability, or a logical FALSE for the probability density function. You can substitute 1 for TRUE and 0 for FALSE if you like.

Finding the Area to the Right of a z Score

For a standardized test with a mean of 500 and a standard deviation of 100, what is the probability that an individual will score above 750, given that the test scores are normally distributed?

First, you calculate the z score by typing

```
=STANDARDIZE(750,500,100)
```

in a blank cell of the worksheet and pressing **<Enter>**. The value of z is 2.5. In this case, you are looking for a right-tailed ("above 750") probability. Remembering that probabilities sum to 1, and that the area to the left of z is found by the function NORM.S.DIST(z), you can use subtraction to find the area to the right of z. To determine the area to the right (beyond) a z score of 2.5 (or equivalently a raw score of 750), you can use the following formula in a blank cell of the workbook:

```
= 1 - NORM.S.DIST(2.5,TRUE)
```

This formula instantly returns the value 0.006209665.

To illustrate further, examine the z scores, the area to the left, and the area to the right of z for our hypothetical test scores from Table 2-7 in Chapter 2 (see Figure 4-5). See that the total is always 1, because we are capturing the entire area under the normal curve.

	A	B	C	D	E	F
1						
2		Scores	z score	Left	Right	Total
3		52	-2.80	0.0026	0.9974	1.0000
4		59	-1.87	0.0304	0.9696	1.0000
5		62	-1.48	0.0695	0.9305	1.0000
6		67	-0.82	0.2059	0.7941	1.0000
7		67	-0.82	0.2059	0.7941	1.0000
8		67	-0.82	0.2059	0.7941	1.0000
9		67	-0.82	0.2059	0.7941	1.0000
10		67	-0.82	0.2059	0.7941	1.0000
11		69	-0.56	0.2887	0.7113	1.0000
12		69	-0.56	0.2887	0.7113	1.0000
13		70	-0.43	0.3353	0.6647	1.0000
14		70	-0.43	0.3353	0.6647	1.0000
15		72	-0.16	0.4357	0.5643	1.0000
16		72	-0.16	0.4357	0.5643	1.0000
17		72	-0.16	0.4357	0.5643	1.0000
18		72	-0.16	0.4357	0.5643	1.0000
19		72	-0.16	0.4357	0.5643	1.0000
20		73	-0.03	0.4880	0.5120	1.0000
21		73	-0.03	0.4880	0.5120	1.0000
22		73	-0.03	0.4880	0.5120	1.0000
23		74	0.10	0.5405	0.4595	1.0000
24		74	0.10	0.5405	0.4595	1.0000
25		75	0.23	0.5923	0.4077	1.0000
26		75	0.23	0.5923	0.4077	1.0000
27		76	0.37	0.6425	0.3575	1.0000
28		78	0.63	0.7352	0.2648	1.0000
29		80	0.89	0.8139	0.1861	1.0000
30		81	1.02	0.8471	0.1529	1.0000
31		81	1.02	0.8471	0.1529	1.0000
32		82	1.16	0.8761	0.1239	1.0000
33		82	1.16	0.8761	0.1239	1.0000
34		83	1.29	0.9011	0.0989	1.0000
35		85	1.55	0.9396	0.0604	1.0000
36		85	1.55	0.9396	0.0604	1.0000
37		87	1.81	0.9652	0.0348	1.0000
38						

Figure 4-5. The z scores, area to the left, and area to the right of z for the hypothetical test scores

Determining the Area Between two z Scores

You can also use a subtraction strategy to find the area between two z scores. For example, just to prove the obvious point, you can find that 95 percent of the standard normal distribution lies between $z = \pm 1.960$ approximately. Enter the following simple formula into any blank worksheet cell:

```
=NORM.S.DIST(1.96, TRUE) - NORM.S.DIST(-1.96, TRUE)
```

If you have Excel 2007 or earlier, type:

```
NORMSDIST(1.96) - NORMSDIST(-1.96)
```

When you press **<Enter>**, **<Tab>**, or click on a different cell, the result 0.95000421 appears in the cell. Of course, your formula will display in the Formula Bar.

This helpful strategy can be used to find the area in any normal distribution between two raw score values. Simply convert each score to a *z* score, and then subtract the cumulative probability for the lower *z* score from the cumulative probability for the higher *z* score. This is the essential nature of a confidence interval, as discussed earlier, finding an upper and a lower limit with a known probability between the two limits.

Finding the z Score for a Given Probability

You have already seen the `NORM.S.INV` function. It is the "inverse" of the standard cumulative normal distribution. You supply a probability, and the function returns the *z* score for that particular probability. This will be the *z* score that divides the standard normal distribution into two areas, *p* (the supplied probability) and $1 - p$ the remainder of the area under the standard normal curve, which must total to 1 by definition. For example, you may want to know the *z* score that divides the upper 7.76 percent of the standard normal distribution from the lower 92.24 percent. You would supply the value .9224 as the argument by typing

```
= NORM.S.INV(0.9224)
```

into a blank cell of your worksheet, and you would instantly find the answer to be $z \approx 1.42$. If you wanted the lower critical value for separating the bottom 7.76 percent of the standard normal distribution from the upper 92.24 percent, you would type

```
= NORM.S.INV(0.0776)
```

and find the answer to be $z \approx -1.42$.

As a reminder, this function can easily be used to find one- and two-tailed critical values of *z*. For example, the critical values for a two-tailed test with alpha = .01 will be found by dividing alpha in half. So you can find the upper limit by using the function

```
= NORM.S.INV(.995)
```

and the lower limit by typing

```
= NORM.S.INV(.005)
```

With .005 of the total area in each tail of the distribution, you are left with .99 in the center between the critical values, which are $z \approx \pm 2.576$. To find the critical value for a one-tailed test in the left tail of the distribution, just type in

```
=NORM.S.INV(alpha)
```

and to find the critical value for a one-tailed test in the right tail of the distribution, type in

```
=NORM.S.INV(1 - alpha)
```

Supply the desired values for alpha and 1 – alpha.

THE BOTTOM LINE
- To find the *z* score for any value of *x*, use `STANDARDIZE(X, Mean, Std_Dev)`.
- To find the area to the left of a *z* score in the standard normal distribution, use `NORM.S.DIST(z,TRUE)`.
- To find the area to the right of a *z* score, use `1 - NORM.S.DIST(z,TRUE)`.
- To find the area between two *z* scores where *z1*< *z2*, use `NORM.S.DIST(z2,TRUE) - NORM.S.DIST(z1,TRUE)`.
- To find the *z* score associated with a given probability, use `NORM.S.INV(p)`.

Comparing Empirical and Theoretical Probabilities

Another common use of the standard normal curve is to give theoretical probabilities, that is, the areas you would expect to see if the data were normally distributed. You can then compare these expected values to the areas that we actually observe in the data.

When you use the `NORM.S.DIST` and `NORM.S.INV` functions, you are assuming that the data are approximately normally distributed. When the data are not normally distributed, the normal probabilities may not be very close to the observed probabilities. But even when the data are decidedly non-normal, the more generous limits of the Chebyshev Inequality will always apply. Return to the CEO ages discussed earlier in the chapter and use the table you learned in Chapter 3 to determine some observed probabilities and compare them to the ones you would expect if the ages were normally distributed. The ages appear to be roughly normally distributed (see Figure 4-6), so the two probabilities should be close to each other.

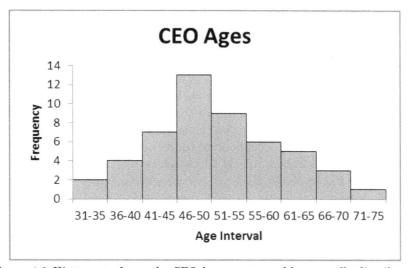

Figure 4-6. Histogram shows the CEOs' ages are roughly normally distributed

By the Empirical Rule, if the ages are normally distributed, approximately 68 percent of observations will be between ±1 standard deviation units (or *z* scores of ±1) of the mean. You could manually count the number of observations with *z* scores between −1 and +1. This would be a laborious and error-prone task if you did it by hand. The Total Row and number filtering features of the table make the task faster, easier, and more accurate.

	Sex ▾	Industry ▾	Age ▾	zAge ▾	Salary ▾	F
42	0	3	32	-2.06	370	
43	0	1	51	-0.04	536	
44	0	3	50	-0.15	291	
45	0	1	40	-1.21	808	
46	0	3	61	1.02	543	
47	0	3	56	0.49	350	
48	0	1	45	-0.68	242	
49	0	3	61	1.02	467	
50	0	2	59	0.81	317	
51	0	3	57	0.60	317	
52	Total			50 ▾	396.56	
53				None		
54				Average		
55				Count		
56				Count Numb		
57				Max		
58				Min		
				Sum		
59				StdDev		
60				Var		
				More Functi‹		

Figure 4-7. CEO Table with Total Row (partial data)

To examine the empirical probability and compare it with the expected probability, open the CEO data again, convert the data to a table, and then add a Total Row (see Figure 4-7). For column E, set the Total Row to display the count of the selected *z* scores by clicking on the dropdown arrow at the right of the field in the Total Row. Note that you can also sort or filter one or more columns without using a table by selecting **Home > Editing > Sort & Filter** or **Data > Sort & Filter > Filter**. Filtering data this way will not allow you to use a Total Row, however.

You can use the filtering abilities of the Excel table to examine the empirical probabilities by working with the column of *z* scores. Set the upper and lower limits as −1 and +1 as described above, and filter the data to count how many of the 50 CEOs have ages between these two limits. In the row of column headings, click on the dropdown arrow at the right of the *zAge* column (see Figure 4-8). Select **Number Filters** and **Between**. When you click on **Between**, you will open a Custom AutoFilter dialog box (Figure 4-9). Type the desired limits as shown in Figure 4-8, and then click **OK.** In the **Total Row,** notice that there are 34 CEOs whose ages are between ±1 standard deviations of the mean (see Figure 4-10). Because the ages are roughly normal, the empirical probability 34/50 = .68 agrees very closely with the theoretical probability in this particular instance.

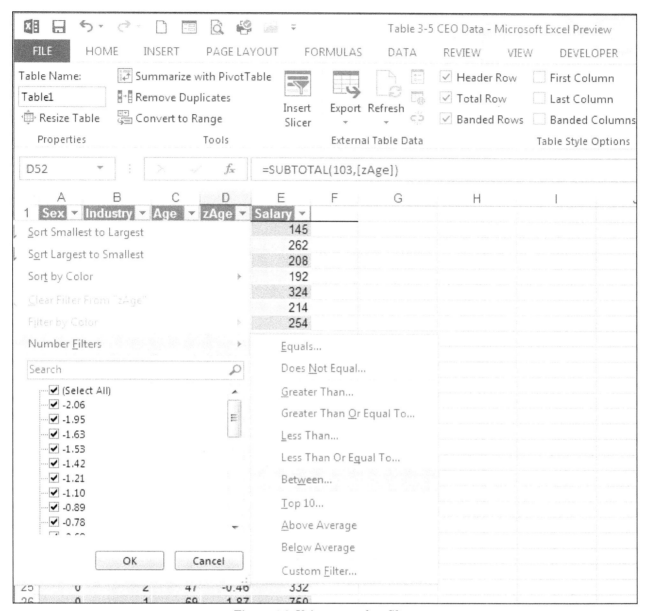

Figure 4-8. Using a number filter

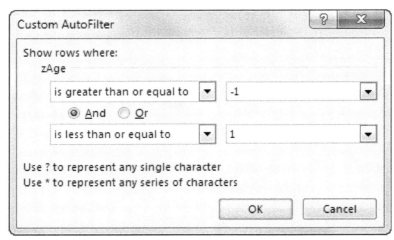

Figure 4-9. Custom AutoFilter dialog

	Sex ▼	Industry ▼	Age ▼	zAge ▼	Salary ▼	F
37	0	2	47	-0.46	862	
38	0	1	48	-0.36	298	
41	0	1	60	0.91	726	
43	0	1	51	-0.04	536	
44	0	3	50	-0.15	291	
47	0	3	56	0.49	350	
48	0	1	45	-0.68	242	
50	0	2	59	0.81	317	
51	0	3	57	0.60	317	
52	Total			34 ▼	2.0294	
53				None		
54				Average		
55				Count		
56				Count Numb		
57				Max		
58				Min		
59				Sum		
60				StdDev		
61				Var		
				More Functi		

Figure 4-10. Counting the result of applying the custom filter (partial data)

Observe in Figure 4-10 that the rows for records 39, 40, 42, 45, 46, and 59 are "missing" from the filtered table. Although the records for these CEOs are hidden from view, they are still present in the data set, and will reappear when the filter is removed. As a visible indicator that the filter is "on," notice the little funnel icon at the right side of the column header row (row 1) for *zAge* in column E. To remove the filter, click on that funnel icon and then click on **Clear Filter from "zAge."** You just found the observed frequency between two *z* scores. You could obviously use this same approach to find observed frequencies to the right of a *z* score or to the left of a *z* score as well. Look again at Figure 4-8 for the wide variety of filtering options.

The discussion of chi-square tests in Chapter 9 revisits observed and expected frequencies for normally distributed data. You will see the tools you learned in this chapter used again there.

THE BOTTOM LINE
- You can use number filters to determine empirical counts in order to compare these counts with theoretical probabilities based on the standard normal distribution.
- Using a table allows you to summarize filtered data with a Total Row.
- When your data are in a table, you access the number filters by clicking on the dropdown arrow at the right of the column label.
- You can also filter data without using a table by selecting **Home > Editing > Sort & Filter** or **Data > Sort & Filter > Filter**.

Chapter 4 Exercises

1. A normal distribution has a mean of 75 with a standard deviation of 10.
   b. About what percent of observations are greater than 95?
   c. About what percent of observations are lower than 65?
   d. About what percent of observations are between 60 and 90?

2. A normal distribution has a mean of 20 and a standard deviation of 4.
   a. Compute the z score associated with a score of 25.
   b. About what percent of observations are lower than 16?
   c. About what percent of observations are higher than 30?
   d. About what percent of observations are between 20 and 25?

3. Assume that the commute time from downtown Chicago to O'Hare Airport using the Chicago Transit Authority train system is normally distributed with a mean of 65 minutes and a standard deviation of 5 minutes.
   a. What is the z score associated with a commute time of 53 minutes?
   b. About what percent of commutes will be faster than 60 minutes?
   c. About what percent of commutes will be longer than 70 minutes?
   d. About what percent of commutes will be between 60 and 70 minutes?

4. Return to the data reported in the worksheet from Table 2-1 on the average wages of covered workers in the 50 states and the District of Columbia. These data are positively skewed (as are most income data). Chebyshev's Inequality states that at least 75% of the data must be between ±2 standard deviations of the mean, while the Empirical Rule states that for a normal distribution approximately 95% of the data will be between ±2 standard deviations. Use the Table's **Total Row** and filtering capabilities to determine which rule better describes the actual percentages for 2001 and 2002 wages.

5 _t_ Tests for One or Two Means

In Chapter 5, you learn how to use Excel for _t_ tests for a single mean, for the means from two independent samples, and for the means from paired samples. As you will see, Excel does not have a built-in one-sample _t_ test, but the computations are simple. Excel provides independent-samples _t_ tests for means from samples with equal and unequal variances, and a paired samples _t_ test.

The _t_ distribution was developed by statistician William S. Gosset (who wrote under the pseudonym "Student") as a way to estimate the "probable error" of the sample mean for small samples, and is thus simply an estimate of _z_ that takes the sample size into account. The _t_ distribution has many similarities to the normal distribution. It is also symmetrical and "bell-shaped," with a mean of zero. However, the standard deviation of the _t_ distribution is larger than 1. Unlike the standard normal distribution, the _t_ distribution is a family of distributions, one for each value of the parameter known as the degrees of freedom, which is based on the sample size. As the degrees of freedom increase, the _t_ distribution becomes closer and closer to the standard normal distribution.

As with the normal distribution, Excel provides a series of functions for determining the probability of an obtained value of _t_ for a given degrees of freedom and number of tails in the hypothesis test. The legacy functions were `TDIST` and `TINV`. Though these functions are still available, the reader should know that the `TDIST` function only works for positive values of _t_. To get around this limitation, you can simply ignore the sign of the value of _t_ by using the `ABS` function. Like the _z_ distribution, the _t_ distribution is symmetrical, so this limitation is not a big one. In fact, in most statistics texts, only the upper halves of both the _z_ and the _t_ distributions are tabled to conserve space.

Excel also provided the "inverse" of the _t_ distribution. By supplying a given probability, the degrees of freedom, and the number of tails in the hypothesis test, the user can find critical value(s) of _t_. This function was called `TINV`, and like `TDIST`, works only with positive values of _t_. These "legacy" functions still work in Excel 2010, but their use is not recommended in Excel 2010. With Excel 2010, Microsoft "fixed" the _t_ distribution functions. The new functions are:

- ☐ `T.DIST(x, deg_freedom,CUMULATIVE)` - Finds the left-tailed probability of _t_
- ☐ `T.DIST.2T(x, deg_freedom)` - Finds the two-tailed probability of _t_
- ☐ `T.DIST.RT(x, deg_freedom)` - Finds the right-tailed probability of _t_
- ☐ `T.DIST.INV(probability, deg_freedom)` - Returns the left-tailed inverse of _t_ for probability
- ☐ `T.DIST.INV.2T(probability, deg_freedom)` - Returns the two-tailed inverse of _t_ for probability

These functions, like their predecessors, work only with values of _t_ that are greater than zero, so you will still have to use the `ABS` function to get the correct result.

The One-Sample *t* Test

The one-sample *t* test is one of the simplest statistical tests. You want to make inferences about the population mean from a single sample of data. To illustrate, consider a manufacturing process that produces nails. Assume that the nails are supposed to be exactly 2.5" in length. At the start of a shift, a sample of 20 nails is collected, and the length of each nail is measured precisely. The production manager wants to be assured before producing an entire batch that the process is producing nails of the desired 2.5" in length, and that any observed departure from 2.5" in the average lengths of the sampled nails is within the tolerance limits for the process and is based on chance (sampling error) alone. If the observed average length of the 20 nails is very different from 2.5", then the manager can conclude that the process is out of control and that adjustments must be made. Assume that the 20 nails averaged 2.5232 inches. in length and that the sample standard deviation was 0.062539 inches. Can you conclude that the sample came from a population with a mean of 2.5 inches? This is an appropriate situation for a one-sample *t* test.

The one-sample *t* test compares a given sample mean, $\bar{x}$, (2.5232 inches in the current case) to a known or hypothesized value of the population mean, μ_0, (2.5 inches in the example) when the population standard deviation σ is unknown. You simply use the sample standard deviation to estimate the population standard deviation. It is especially important to use the *t* test when sample sizes are small. As sample sizes become larger, the sample variance becomes a better and better estimate of the population variance, and the *t* test can easily be replaced by a *z* test.

When the null hypothesis that the sample mean equals the hypothesized value is true, the statistic derived from the equation

$$t = \frac{\bar{x} - \mu_0}{s_{\bar{x}}}$$

is distributed as *t* with $n - 1$ degrees of freedom. The denominator

$$s_{\bar{x}} = \sqrt{\frac{s_x^2}{n}} = \frac{s_x}{\sqrt{n}}$$

is the "standard error of the mean," which is the standard deviation of the sampling distribution of means for samples of size *n*. Recall that Excel reports this value for raw data via the Descriptive Statistics tool. In this case,

$$s_{\bar{x}} = \frac{0.062539}{\sqrt{20}} = 0.0140$$

The hypothesized value of μ_0 is, of course, supplied by the researcher. In the current example,

$$t = \frac{\bar{x} - \mu_0}{s_{\bar{x}}} = \frac{2.5232 - 2.50}{0.0140} = 1.659$$

You evaluate this obtained one-sample *t* for a two-tailed test with $n - 1 = 19$ degrees of freedom. This is easy to do with the T.DIST.2T function:

```
=T.DIST.2T(1.659, 19)
```

The p value is .114, and thus the t test is not significant. You can retain the null hypothesis that the sample mean is not significantly different from 2.5. In practical terms, this result means that the manager can start production of the batch of nails.

Though there is not a tool labeled "one-sample t test" in Excel, the calculations are simple. For those who want to use a built-in procedure, the Z.TEST function can be used for a one-sample t test, as discussed briefly later in this chapter. As illustrated in Appendix D, MegaStat does provide both one-sample t tests and one-sample z tests for summary data and raw data. In reality, using the simple formula shown above to find t is just as easy.

Example Data

The body temperature measurements of 130 healthy adults were recorded (see Table 5-1).[1] Test the hypothesis that these 130 observations came from a population with a mean body temperature of 98.6 degrees Fahrenheit. The belief that the average normal temperature of a human is 98.6 degrees Fahrenheit is a "fact" people have accepted for more than a century. But is it really true? You can retrieve the file from the book's companion web site. That file also includes the participant's sex (1 = *male* and 2 = *female*) and pulse rate.

Table 5-1. Body temperature measurements for 130 healthy adults

Body Temp				
96.3	98.0	98.7	97.9	98.6
96.7	98.0	98.8	97.9	98.7
96.9	98.0	98.8	98.0	98.7
97.0	98.0	98.8	98.0	98.7
97.1	98.0	98.9	98.0	98.7
97.1	98.1	99.0	98.0	98.7
97.1	98.1	99.0	98.0	98.7
97.2	98.2	99.0	98.1	98.8
97.3	98.2	99.1	98.2	98.8
97.4	98.2	99.2	98.2	98.8
97.4	98.2	99.3	98.2	98.8
97.4	98.3	99.4	98.2	98.8
97.4	98.3	99.5	98.2	98.8
97.5	98.4	96.4	98.2	98.8
97.5	98.4	96.7	98.3	98.9
97.6	98.4	96.8	98.3	99.0
97.6	98.4	97.2	98.3	99.0
97.6	98.5	97.2	98.4	99.1
97.7	98.5	97.4	98.4	99.1
97.8	98.6	97.6	98.4	99.2
97.8	98.6	97.7	98.4	99.2
97.8	98.6	97.7	98.4	99.3
97.8	98.6	97.8	98.5	99.4
97.9	98.6	97.8	98.6	99.9
97.9	98.6	97.8	98.6	100.0
98.0	98.7	97.9	98.6	100.8

---

[1]   These data were published by Dr. Alan Shoemaker of Calvin College and are used with his permission.

Using Excel for a One-Sample t Test

Let us use the Descriptive Statistics tool in the Analysis ToolPak to find the mean, standard deviation, and the standard error of the mean for the 130 body temperatures. Remember to select **Data > Analysis > Data Analysis > Descriptive Statistics**. The results are shown in Table 5-2.

Table 5-2. Descriptive statistics for body temperature data

Temp	
Mean	98.25
Standard Error	0.0643
Median	98.3
Mode	98
Standard Deviation	0.7332
Sample Variance	0.5376
Kurtosis	0.78
Skewness	0.00
Range	4.5
Minimum	96.3
Maximum	100.8
Sum	12772.4
Count	130
Confidence Level(95.0%)	0.13

Using some calculations with the formula for the one-sample *t* test, we obtain the following value of *t*:

$$t = \frac{\overline{x} - \mu_0}{s_{\overline{x}}} = \frac{98.25 - 98.6}{.0643} = -5.45$$

When you use the same formula or function repetitively, you may want to create a worksheet template. With such a template, you can enter new data, but keep using the same formulas and functions each time you need to do a new analysis. In the following general worksheet template model for a one-sample *t* test, one enters the raw data values in column E. Figure 5-1 reveals the formulas used to calculate the value of *t*, the standard deviation, and the standard error of the mean, as well as the one- and two-tailed probabilities of the obtained *t*. Note in cells C9 to C11 that the ABS function is used to find the probability of the obtained *t* because the *t* distributions functions work only for nonnegative values, as discussed previously. Just to make things a little prettier, the conditional IF statements keep the cells blank when there are no data in the data-entry area. Examine the formulas and functions carefully to see that the template counts the number of data entries, calculates the sample mean, calculates the standard deviation, and then calculates the standard error of the mean. The template then calculates the value of *t* and the degrees of freedom. Next, the template reports the two-tailed, left-tailed, and right-tailed probabilities of *t*, calculates Cohen's *d* (see below), and then calculates the mean difference and a 95% confidence interval for the mean difference. Similar output is typically produced by such statistics packages as SPSS and SAS, but one must understand how to read the output for it to be of any use.

▲	A	B	C
1			
2		Sample Size	=IF(E3<>"",COUNT(data),"")
3		Population Mean	
4		Sample Mean	=IF(E3<>"",AVERAGE(data),"")
5		Standard Deviation	=IF(E3<>"",STDEV.S(data),"")
6		Standard Error	=IF(ISNUMBER(C5),C5/SQRT(C2),"")
7		*t*	=IF(ISNUMBER(C2),(C4-C3)/C6,"")
8		*df*	=IF(ISNUMBER(C2),C2-1,"")
9		Two-tailed Probability	=IF(ISNUMBER(C7),T.DIST.2T(ABS(C7),C8),"")
10		Left-tailed Probability	=IF(ISNUMBER(C7),T.DIST(ABS(C7),C8,TRUE),"")
11		Right-tailed Probability	=IF(ISNUMBER(C7),T.DIST.RT(ABS(C7),C8),"")
12		Cohen's *d*	=IF(ISNUMBER(C7),(C4-C3)/C5,"")
13		Mean Difference	=IF(ISNUMBER(C2),C4-C3,"")
14		95% Confidence Interval	
15		Lower Limit	Upper Limit
16		=IF(ISNUMBER(C13),C13-T.INV.2T(0.05,C8)*C6,"")	=IF(ISNUMBER(C13),C13+T.INV.2T(0.05,C8)*C6,"")

Figure 5-1. Worksheet model for the one-sample *t* test

The user must decide whether the results are in the hypothesized direction before determining the appropriateness of a two-tailed, left-tailed, or right-tailed test. This worksheet template is freely available for personal and educational use and can be obtained from the companion web page. Figure 5-2 shows the template ready for data entry.

⊿	A	B	C	D	E	F
1						
2		Sample Size			Data	
3		Population Mean				
4		Sample Mean				
5		Standard Deviation				
6		Standard Error				
7		*t*				
8		*df*				
9		Two-tailed Probability				
10		Left-tailed Probability				
11		Right-tailed Probability				
12		Cohen's *d*				
13		Mean Difference				
14		95% Confidence Interval				
15		Lower Limit	Upper Limit			
16						
17						
18		**Instructions for Using this Template:**				
19						
20		Enter the hypothesized population mean μ_0				
21		in cell C3. To remove the data validation box for				
22		cell C3, press the <Esc> key or select a different				
23		cell.				
24						
25		Enter up to 500 observed data values in the				
26		date entry area in column E, beginning with cell				
27		E3.				
28		This template performs a one-sample *t* test and				
29		calculates the probability that the sample came				
30		from a population with a mean of μ_0.				
31						
32		The template is protected to keep the user from				
33		deleting the formulas. However, you can easily				
34		see the formulas used to calculate the results by				
35		placing the cursor pointer in the light-orange				
36		shaded cells.				
37		This template is copyright (c) 2012 by				
38		Larry A. Pace, Ph.D. All rights are reserved.				
39		Personal and educational use are freely granted.				

Figure 5-2. One-sample *t* test worksheet template ready for data entry

The one-sample t test performed by the worksheet template appears in Figure 5-3. Simply copy and paste the 130 temperatures into column D, and type 98.6 as the test value in cell B2. When you press <Enter>, the template does the rest. Note the use of scientific notation to report the p values, because they are very small. The two-tailed probability is .000000120532, which is far less than .001. The publication manual of the American Psychological Association (APA, 2010) informs us that the lowest probability we should report is $p = .001$, and that if the probability is less than .001, we should report it as $p < .001$. If you are interested in reading more about how to format statistics in proper APA style, I devote a chapter to that subject in my new book *Using Microsoft Word to Write Research Papers in APA Style* (Pace, 2012c). The APA manual also tells us we should report confidence intervals and an effect-size index for each hypothesis test. In this case, we are using Cohen's d, which is a commonly reported index of effect size for t tests. Note the fact that zero or no difference is not "in" the 95% confidence interval is another indication that we should reject the null hypothesis that this sample came from a population with a mean body temperature of 98.6 degrees Fahrenheit.

	A	B	C	D	E	F
1						
2		Sample Size	130		Data	
3		Population Mean	98.6		96.3	
4		Sample Mean	98.24923077		96.7	
5		Standard Deviation	0.733183158		96.9	
6		Standard Error	0.064304417		97	
7		t	-5.454823292		97.1	
8		df	129		97.1	
9		Two-tailed Probability	2.41063E-07		97.1	
10		Left-tailed Probability	0.999999879		97.2	
11		Right-tailed Probability	1.20532E-07		97.3	
12		Cohen's d	-0.478419651		97.4	
13		Mean Difference	-0.350769231		97.4	
14		95% Confidence Interval			97.4	
15		Lower Limit	Upper Limit		97.4	
16		-0.477997094	-0.223541367		97.5	
17					97.5	

Figure 5-3. One-sample t test results

For the sake of comparison, examine the output from SPSS for the same one-sample t test (Figure 5-4), followed by the output from the statistical programming language R (Figure 5-5). Unsurprisingly, all three technologies produce equivalent results. The template and R report the p value in scientific notation, while SPSS reports it as .000. Inscrutably, SPSS uses the abbreviation "Sig." for significance. The p value is very low, but it is not exactly zero. As discussed above, APA style requires this value to be reported as $p < .001$.

One-Sample Statistics

	N	Mean	Std. Deviation	Std. Error Mean
Body Temperature	130	98.25	.733	.064

One-Sample Test

	Test Value = 98.6					
					95% Confidence Interval of the Difference	
				Mean		
	t	df	Sig. (2-tailed)	Difference	Lower	Upper
Body Temperature	-5.455	129	.000	-.351	-.48	-.22

Figure 5-4. SPSS output for a one-sample *t* test with the body temperature data

```
          One Sample t-test

data:  Temp
t = -5.4548, df = 129, p-value = 2.411e-07
alternative hypothesis: true mean is not equal to 98.6
95 percent confidence interval:
 98.12200 98.37646
sample estimates:
mean of x
 98.24923
```

Figure 5-5. R output for the one-sample *t* test

Observe that SPSS produces the same confidence interval as the Excel template does, and that R reports the same *p* value as the template, but reports the confidence interval for the mean, rather than the mean difference.

We conclude that the probability that the 130 adults came from a population with a mean body temperature of 98.6 degrees Fahrenheit is less than one in 1,000, $M = 98.25$, $SD = 0.733$, $t(129) = -5.45$, $p < .001$, two-tailed, $d = 0.48$, 95% CI[−0.48, −0.22]. One could conclude either that the sample is atypically cooler than average, or more realistically that the true population mean temperature is not 98.6. Interestingly, other studies have shown that the true population mean of normal human body temperature is probably closer to 98.2 than to 98.6.

It can be mentioned in passing that although Excel does not label it as such, the one-sample ZTEST function in Excel makes use of the sample standard deviation when raw data are used and the value of the population standard deviation is omitted. Therefore, Excel performs a one-sample *t* test in that particular case. By naming the range of data, entering the hypothesized mean, and omitting the population standard deviation, you are actually finding *t* rather than *z*. With the data range named "data", the following formula will produce the same result as the multiple formulas and functions shown in Figure 5-1.

=NORM.S.INV(1-Z.TEST(data,98.6))

This formula will find the value of *t* rather than z because we are using the sample standard deviation for our calculations. Then it is easy to use the *t* distribution functions to find the probability for a given number of tails and degrees of freedom. For example, assuming that the formula shown above is in cell G2:

$$=T.DIST.2T(ABS(G2),129)$$

Remember that the *t* distribution functions works only for positive values of *t*, thus the need for the ABS function above. Here is the result of using the Z.TEST function with the raw data, and you see that it produces exactly the same results as the other approaches (Figure 5-6).

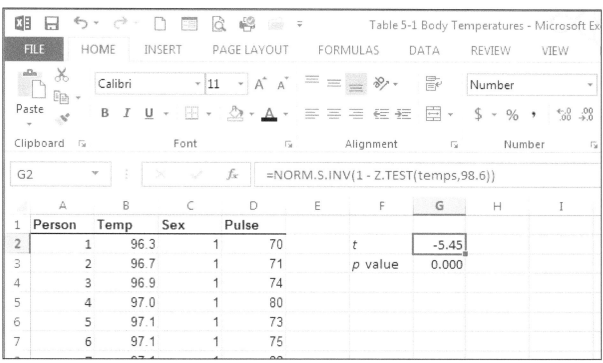

Figure 5-6. Z.TEST function produces the same results as the other approaches

---

THE BOTTOM LINE
- The one-sample *t* test compares a sample mean to a population mean when sample sizes are small and when the population variance is not known.
- Excel does not provide a one-sample *t* test.
- The TDIST and TINV functions only work for positive values of *t*.
- The ZTEST function actually does a one-sample *t* test when the population variance is omitted.

Independent-Samples *t* Test

The independent-samples *t* test compares the means from two separate samples. The key to this procedure is that there is no overlap in group membership. Each observation belongs to only one sample. The two samples may represent experimental conditions, such as a control group and an experimental group, or they may represent naturally-occurring groups such as males and females. You are interested in determining whether the observed difference between the sample means is statistically significant, or whether you can only conclude that the observed differences are attributable to sampling error.

It is not required that the two samples have the same number of observations. The Analysis ToolPak performs both one- and two-tailed independent-samples *t* tests. The independent-samples *t* test assumes that the data are ratio or interval, that the observations in each group are independent, that the samples are drawn from normally distributed populations, and that the population variances are equal. When the sample variances are not equal, an adjustment to the degrees of freedom for the *t* test can take this inequality into account. Excel provides *t* tests for both equal variances and unequal variances.

The equal variances test is the more commonly taught of the two tests, but many statisticians prefer to use the unequal variances test in all cases. In the case of two independent groups, a simple *F* test can be used to test the equality of the variances in order to determine which *t* test is appropriate. The ratio of the larger of the two sample variances to the smaller variance is distributed as *F* with n_1 − 1 and n_2 − 1 degrees of freedom. If the *F* ratio is significant at $p < .05$, one should make use of the unequal variances test.

The formula for the independent-samples *t* test for equal variances used by Excel is based on a pooled variance estimate. This value weights the estimate by the relative sizes of the two samples. The value of *t* is calculated as

$$t = \frac{(\bar{x}_1 - \bar{x}_2) - (\mu_1 - \mu_2)}{\sqrt{\left[\frac{(n_1 - 1)s_1^2 + (n_2 - 1)s_2^2}{n_1 + n_2 - 2}\right]\left[\frac{1}{n_1} + \frac{1}{n_2}\right]}}$$

This formula is appropriate when the sample variances are roughly equal. Although the formula looks imposing, it may help to see that the denominator term is the estimated standard error of the difference between means of two independent samples. Recognizing the first part of the term under the radical in the above formula as the pooled variance estimate, s_{pooled}^2, and understanding that the hypothesized mean difference $\mu_1 - \mu_2$ is usually zero, you can use a simpler form:

$$t = \frac{\bar{x}_1 - \bar{x}_2}{s_{pooled}\sqrt{\left(\frac{1}{n_1} + \frac{1}{n_2}\right)}}$$

By this point in their statistics course, even with a simpler presentation of the formula, most learners are happy enough to let a software program find the value of *t* for them.

The unequal variances test makes an adjustment to the degrees of freedom using what is known as the Welch-Satterthwaite formula. This is the formula for *t*:

$$t = \frac{(\bar{x}_1 - \bar{x}_2) - (\mu_1 - \mu_2)}{\sqrt{\frac{s_1^2}{n_1} + \frac{s_2^2}{n_2}}}$$

Here is the formula for the adjusted degrees of freedom:

$$df = \frac{\left(\dfrac{s_1^2}{n_1} + \dfrac{s_2^2}{n_2}\right)^2}{\dfrac{\left(\dfrac{s_1^2}{n_1}\right)^2}{n_1 - 1} + \dfrac{\left(\dfrac{s_2^2}{n_2}\right)^2}{n_2 - 1}}$$

Excel uses the adjustment above, but rounds the degrees of freedom to the nearest integer.

Example Data

The data in Table 5-3 represent psychological need for competence scores on a 100-point scale for selected student leaders and a nonequivalent control group consisting of a randomly selected class of college students at the same university. Use an independent-samples t test to determine whether the two groups have equal need for competence. Because student leaders are expected to express a higher need for competence, perform a one-tailed test. These data are available on the companion web page.

Table 5-3. Need for competence scores

Leaders	Control
78.6	66.7
76.2	71.4
85.7	57.1
81.0	52.4
97.6	57.1
61.9	85.7
88.1	76.2
59.5	64.3
73.8	54.8
57.1	92.9
81.0	73.8
92.9	97.6
83.3	64.3
78.6	69.1
100.0	85.7
88.1	50.0
76.2	69.1
76.2	92.9
78.6	61.9
	61.9
	66.7
	73.8
	85.7

	A	B	C
1	Value	Group	
2	78 6	1	
3	76 2	1	
4	85 7	1	
5	81 0	1	
6	97 6	1	
7	61 9	1	
8	88 1	1	
9	59 5	1	
10	73 8	1	
34	69 1	0	
35	85 7	0	
36	50 0	0	
37	69 1	0	
38	92 9	0	
39	61 9	0	
40	61 9	0	
41	66 7	0	
42	73 8	0	
43	85 7	0	
44			

Figure 5-7. Use of dummy-coding for groups (partial data)

Excel allows you to use side-by-side data like those in Table 5-3 for an independent-samples *t* test. However, some statistics packages such as SPSS require the dependent variable scores to be placed in a single column with an additional column for the grouping variable, which can be an indicator (1, 2) or a dummy-coded (0, 1) column to identify the group to which the observation belongs. This format is called "stacked" data. Figure 5-7 shows the use of dummy-coding with a 1 to represent the leader group and 0 to represent the randomly-selected class. Clearly, you could still use named ranges with such a coding scheme in Excel. Many instructors prefer the stacked coding with indicator variables because they use a statistical package in combination with Excel. In addition to compatibility with other programs, another advantage of the column of group membership codes is that it makes sorting and filtering the data easier. For now, we will just leave the columns side-by-side with appropriate labels (see Figure 5-8).

	A	B	C
1	Leaders	Control	
2	78 6	66 7	
3	76 2	71 4	
4	85 7	57 1	
5	81 0	52 4	
6	97 6	57 1	
7	61 9	85 7	
8	88 1	76 2	
9	59 5	64 3	
10	73 8	54 8	
11	57 1	92 9	
12	81 0	73 8	
13	92 9	97 6	
14	83 3	64 3	
15	78 6	69 1	
16	100 0	85 7	
17	88 1	50 0	
18	76 2	69 1	
19	76 2	92 9	
20	78 6	61 9	
21		61 9	
22		66 7	
23		73 8	
24		85 7	

Figure 5-8. Data in Excel

The Independent-Samples *t* Test in the Analysis ToolPak

First check the homogeneity of variance assumption by using the F-Test tool in the Analysis ToolPak (**Data > Analysis > Data Analysis > F-Test Two-Sample for Variances**). Though it is technically not necessary, when using this tool, it helps to divide the larger sample variance by the smaller one in order to make the F ratio greater than one. To ensure this, assign the scores for the control class to Variable 1 and the scores for the leaders to Variable 2. The FTEST dialog appears in Figure 5-9, and the test results in Figure 5-10. The lack of significance for the obtained F ratio indicates that the equal variances test is appropriate.

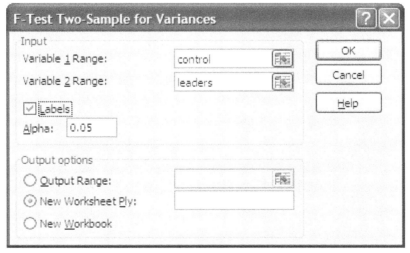

Figure 5-9. F-Test dialog box

	A	B	C
1	F-Test Two-Sample for Variances		
2			
3		Control	Leaders
4	Mean	70.9173913	79.70526316
5	Variance	186.0542292	133.9460819
6	Observations	23	19
7	df	22	18
8	F	1.389023304	
9	P(F<=f) one-tail	0.241517509	
10	F Critical one-tail	2.168473511	
11			

Figure 5-10. Nonsignificant *F* ratio indicates variances are approximately equal

To perform the independent-samples *t* test, select **Data > Analysis > Data Analysis > t-test: Two-Sample Assuming Equal Variances**. Click **OK** and the *t* test Dialog Box appears (Figure 5-11). Supply the ranges for the two variables, including labels if desired. Click **OK** to run the *t* test. The resulting *t* test output appears in a new worksheet (see Table 5-4).

The significant *t* test indicates that you can reject the null hypothesis that student leaders and the nonequivalent control group have the same psychological need for competence. Because the hypothesis was directional, a one-tailed test is appropriate. Student leaders expressed higher levels of need for competence than did randomly selected students, $t(40) = 2.22$, $p = .016$, one-tailed. As the Analysis ToolPak provides a complete and well-labeled independent-samples *t* test, no worksheet template will be discussed here, though for the inquisitive, there is one available at the companion web site. It works in a fashion similar to the one-sample *t* test template discussed earlier, and provides an effect size index as well as a confidence interval for the mean difference.

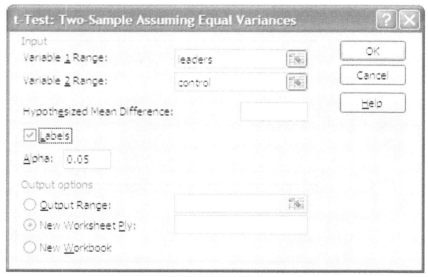

Figure 5-11. Independent-samples *t* test dialog box

Table 5-4. Output from _t_ test

t-Test: Two-Sample Assuming Equal Variances

	Leaders	Control
Mean	79.705	70.917
Variance	133.946	186.054
Observations	19	23
Pooled Variance	162.606	
Hypothesized Mean Difference	0	
df	40	
t Stat	2.223	
P(T<=t) one-tail	0.016	
t Critical one-tail	1.684	
P(T<=t) two-tail	0.032	
t Critical two-tail	2.021	

For comparison purposes, here is the output from the unequal-variances _t_ test (see Table 5-5). The MegaStat add-in (Appendix D) calculates the same value of _t_ as the Analysis ToolPak, but reports the degrees of freedom as 39, rounding down rather than up. The actual value of degrees of freedom using the Welch-Satterthwaite formula is 39.96.

Table 5-5. Output from the Unequal-Variances _t_ test

t-Test: Two-Sample Assuming Unequal Variances

	Leaders	Control
Mean	79.705	70.917
Variance	133.946	186.054
Observations	19	23
Hypothesized Mean Difference	0	
df	40	
t Stat	2.259	
P(T<=t) one-tail	0.015	
t Critical one-tail	1.684	
P(T<=t) two-tail	0.029	
t Critical two-tail	2.021	

Confidence Intervals for the Independent-Samples _t_ Test

Most statistical software packages provide a confidence interval for the mean difference when reporting the results of an independent-samples _t_ test. Excel does not provide this feature, but the MegaStat add-in discussed in Appendix D does. To calculate the confidence interval, we find the standard error of the mean difference, and then multiply that value by a critical value of _t_ for the desired confidence level. This margin of error is subtracted from the mean difference for the lower limit and added to the mean difference for the upper limit. Here is the formula.

$$CI = (\overline{x}_1 - \overline{x}_2) \pm t_{\alpha/2}\left(s_{pooled} \times \sqrt{\left(\frac{1}{n_1} + \frac{1}{n_2}\right)}\right)$$

Let us develop a 95% confidence interval for the mean difference between the leaders' and non-leaders' need for competence scores. The critical value of t with $n_1 + n_2 - 2 = 19 + 23 - 2 = 40$ degrees of freedom is found using the T.INV.2T function.

$$=\text{T.INV.2T}(0.05,40)= 2.021$$

The pooled standard deviation is the square root of the pooled variance reported by Excel's Analysis ToolPak, $s_{pooled} = \sqrt{162.606} = 12.7517$.

$$95\%CI = (79.705 - 70.917) \pm 2.021\left(12.7517 \times \sqrt{\left(\frac{1}{19} + \frac{1}{23}\right)}\right)$$

$$= 8.7879 \pm 2.021\left(12.7517 \times \sqrt{0.09611}\right)$$

$$= 8.7879 \pm 2.021\left(12.7517 \times 0.310016\right)$$

$$-8.7879 \pm 2.021(3.953226)$$

$$= 8.7879 \pm 7.989469$$

$$= 0.7984, 16.7773$$

Apart from rounding error, these manual calculations produce the same confidence interval as does MegaStat, which reports the confidence interval as (0.7981, 16.7776). The APA format for reporting this confidence interval is 95%CI [0.7981, 16.7776].

THE BOTTOM LINE

☐ The independent-samples *t* test compares the means from two separate groups.

☐ The *t* test assumes interval or ratio data, normality of population distribution, homogeneity of variance, and independence of the observations within the groups.

☐ Place the data in side-by-side columns or use named ranges.

☐ You can test the homogeneity of variance by using the F-Test tool (**Data > Analysis > Data Analysis > F-Test Two-Sample for Variances**).

☐ To perform the independent-samples t test when the variances are equal, select **Data > Analysis > Data Analysis > t-Test: Two-Sample Assuming Equal Variances**.

☐ Enter the appropriate information and Click **OK** to run the t test.

☐ The Analysis ToolPak does not provide a confidence interval for the mean difference, but MegaStat does.

Paired-Samples *t* Test

The dependent or paired-samples *t* test is applied to data in which the observations from one sample are paired with or linked to the observations in the second sample. An obvious example is before and after measurements such as a pretest and a posttest for the same individuals. Another example would include scores from naturally-occurring pairs such as twins or mothers and daughters. A less obvious example is the use of matching to create groups that are as similar to each other as possible by assigning subjects or participants to the groups based on one or more variables. The paired-samples *t* test assumes that the data are interval or ratio, that the separate observations within each group are independent, and that the differences between the two scores for each pair are normally distributed.

Earlier computing forms for the paired samples t test were based on the correlation between the two sets of scores and required the computation of the correlation coefficient. Most modern texts use the direct difference method, which is computationally much simpler. To calculate t, create a column for the differences between the paired measurements. Because the differences are based on the two measures, they are not constrained to have a mean of zero. They will have a mean of zero only when, on average, there are no differences between the two measurements. Take this column of difference scores, and calculate its mean, standard deviation, and standard error. Of course, the simplest way to do that is to use the Descriptive Statistics tool in the Analysis ToolPak. Then the value of t can be readily found as

$$t = \frac{\overline{x}_D}{s_{\overline{x}_D}}$$

where $\overline{x}_D$ is the average difference, and $s_{\overline{x}_D}$ is the standard error of the mean difference, found by dividing the standard deviation of the difference scores by the square root of n, the number of pairs of observations. The similarity of this formula to that of the one-sample t should be obvious. When the null hypothesis that the average difference is zero is true, the value obtained above is distributed as t with $n - 1$ degrees of freedom. It is very easy to conceive the paired-samples t test as a special case of the one-sample t test, and the one-sample t test worksheet template introduced earlier can be used for this test by entering the column of difference scores as the data values and 0 or no difference on average as the test value ("population mean").

Excel provides a well-labeled and accurate paired-samples t test tool via the Analysis ToolPak, as discussed below. A paired-samples t test worksheet template is also available at the companion web page.

Example Data

Table 5-6. Attitudes toward Statistics

Student	Time1	Time2
1	84	88
2	45	54
3	32	43
4	48	42
5	53	51
6	64	73
7	45	58
8	74	79
9	68	72
10	54	52
11	90	92
12	84	89
13	72	82
14	69	82
15	72	73

Fifteen students completed an Attitude toward Statistics (ATS) scale at the beginning and at the end of a basic statistics course (data collected by the author). The data are as shown in Table 5-6 and are available on the companion web page. Higher scores indicate more favorable attitudes toward statistics. You want to test the hypothesis that the ATS score after the statistics course is significantly higher (one-tailed) than the score at the beginning. Let us adopt an alpha level of .05. The data entered in Excel appear in Figure 5-12.

	A	B	C
1	Student	Time1	Time2
2	1	84	88
3	2	45	54
4	3	32	43
5	4	48	42
6	5	53	51
7	6	64	73
8	7	45	58
9	8	74	79
10	9	68	72
11	10	54	52
12	11	90	92
13	12	84	89
14	13	72	82
15	14	69	82
16	15	72	73

Figure 5-12. Data for paired-samples *t* test

Paired-Samples *t* Test in the Analysis ToolPak

To perform the analysis, select **Data > Analysis > Data Analysis > t-Test: Paired Two Sample for Means**. The dialog box is shown in Figure 5-13. Enter the Variable1 and Variable2 ranges as shown. If you did not name your ranges, you can just enter the cell references or drag through the data. You may place the output in a new worksheet or in the same worksheet as the data. In this case, keep the default and select a new worksheet (see Figure 5-13). The output table for the paired-samples *t* test appears in Figure 5-14. The calculated *t* statistic of −3.398 indicates that the Time2 ATS score is significantly higher than the ATS score for Time1. Taking a statistics course is associated with significantly more positive attitudes toward statistics after the class is finished, $t(14) = -3.398$, $p = .002$, one-tailed.

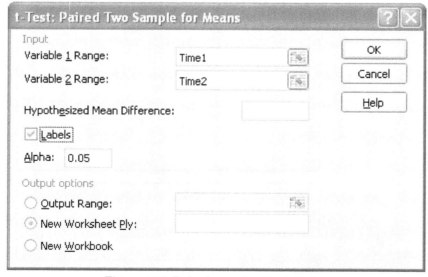

Figure 5-13. Paired-samples *t* test dialog

	A	B	C	D	E	F
1	t-Test: Paired Two Sample for Means					
2						
3		Time1	Time2			
4	Mean	63.6	68.66666667			
5	Variance	283.2571429	295.0952381			
6	Observations	15	15			
7	Pearson Correlation	0.942529541				
8	Hypothesized Mean Difference	0				
9	df	14				
10	t Stat	-3.397852649				
11	P(T<=t) one-tail	0.002165676				
12	t Critical one-tail	1.761310115				
13	P(T<=t) two-tail	0.004331353				
14	t Critical two-tail	2.144786681				
15						

Sheet4 / Sheet1 / Sheet2 / Sheet3

Figure 5-7. Paired-samples t test output

Confidence Intervals for the Paired-Samples t Test

We can develop a confidence interval for the mean difference in the paired-samples t test in a fashion similar to that we used for the one-sample and independent-samples t tests.

We can calculate a column of difference scores. To make our calculations easier, let us subtract the Time 1 score from the Time 2 score. Now, we can calculate the average difference score (which will also be the same as the mean for Time 2 minus the mean for Time 1. More important, we can calculate the standard deviation of the difference scores, and their standard error (the standard deviation divided by the square root of the number of differences). We can use the T.INV.2T function to locate a critical value of t, and then multiply the critical value of t by the standard error of the differences. This produces the margin of error, which we then subtract from the mean difference for the lower limit and add to the mean difference for the upper limit. See the calculations in Figure 5-8, in which some of the equivalent terms from the Analysis ToolPak and the rather simple calculations for the confidence interval are highlighted. The MegaStat add-in (Appendix D) produces an identical confidence interval. An appropriate APA-style summary statement of these results is as follows. A paired-samples t test revealed that attitudes toward statistics after a statistics class ($M = 68.67$, $SD = 17.18$) were significantly more positive than the attitudes before the class ($M = 63.6$, $SD = 16.83$), $t(14) = 3.40$, $p = .004$, 95% CI[1.868, 8,265].

	A	B	C	D	E	F	G	H	I
1	Student	Time1	Time2	Diff		t-Test: Paired Two Sample for Means			
2	1	84	88	4					
3	2	45	54	9			*Time1*	*Time2*	*Difference*
4	3	32	43	11		Mean	63.6	68.66667	5.066666667
5	4	48	42	-6		Variance	283.2571429	295.0952	
6	5	53	51	-2		Observations	15	15	
7	6	64	73	9		Pearson Correlation	0.942529541		
8	7	45	58	13		Hypothesized Mean Difference	0		
9	8	74	79	5		df	14		
10	9	68	72	4		t Stat	-3.397852649		
11	10	54	52	-2		P(T<=t) one-tail	0.002165676		
12	11	90	92	2		t Critical one-tail	1.761310136		
13	12	84	89	5		P(T<=t) two-tail	0.004331353		
14	13	72	82	10		t Critical two-tail	2.144786688		
15	14	69	82	13					
16	15	72	73	1		95% Confidence Interal for the Mean Difference			
17				5.066666667		Mean Difference	5.066666667		
18						Standard Deviation of Differences	5.775152029		
19						Standard Error of Differences	1.491137842		
20						Critical Value of *t*	2.144786688		
21						Margin of error	3.198172593		
22						Lower Limit	1.868494074		
23						Upper Limit	8.26483926		

Figure 5-8. Calculations for a confidence interval for the mean difference

A paired-samples *t* test template is available on the companion web site, and as with the other two *t* tests, provides an effect size index and a confidence interval.

THE BOTTOM LINE
- The paired-samples *t* test compares the means for pairs of observations.
- The paired-samples *t* test assumes interval or ratio data, independence of observations within each group, and that the differences between pairs are normally distributed.
- The paired-samples *t* test can easily be seen as a one-sample (the differences) *t* test.
- Enter data in two columns with appropriate labels.
- Select Data > Analysis > Data Analysis > t-Test: Paired Two Sample for Means.
- Enter data ranges or names for the two variables.
- Check Labels if the data have labels.
- Accept or change the default .05 alpha level.
- Click **OK** to run the paired-samples *t* test.

Effect Size for *t* Tests

There are several effect size indexes for the *t* test. One of the most popular and easiest to compute and interpret is Cohen's *d* (Cohen, 1988), which is a standardized effect size index calculated in standard deviation units. For the independent-samples *t* test, *d* can be calculated as

$$d = \frac{\overline{x}_1 - \overline{x}_2}{s_{pooled}}$$

Although Excel does not compute effect size indexes automatically, the calculations are trivial. Remember that for the equal-variances t test, Excel's Analysis ToolPak reports the pooled variance estimate (see Table 5-4, page 115), so the square root of that value is the pooled standard deviation. For the paired-samples t test, one could calculate a value of d as follows:

$$d = \frac{\overline{x}_D}{s_D}$$

Finally, for the one-sample t test, the value of d can be found from the following formula:

$$d = \frac{\overline{x} - \mu_0}{s}$$

Cohen suggests these guidelines for interpreting the magnitude of the effect (see Table 5-7).

Table 5-7. Guidelines for interpreting Cohen's d

Value of d	Size of Effect
.20	Small
.50	Medium
.80	Large

THE BOTTOM LINE
- Cohen's d is a popular effect size index for t tests.
- Cohen's d is a standardized effect size index that expresses the magnitude of a difference or effect in standard deviation units.
- The mean difference divided by the standard deviation (or pooled standard deviation) is Cohen's d.

Chapter 5 Exercises

1. Using the data set from Table 2-1, conduct a one-sample t test of the one-tailed hypothesis that the average percent change in wages from 2001 to 2002 was greater than zero. Calculate and interpret Cohen's d as a measure of effect size.

2. Using the same data set, conduct a paired-samples t test to compare the average wages in 2001 and 2002. Test the one-tailed hypothesis that the average wages for 2002 are higher than the average wages for 2001. Calculate and interpret Cohen's d as a measure of effect size. Compare your results to those of the one-sample t test you just performed.

3. From the companion web page, obtain the expanded worksheet file for Table 5-1, in which sex is coded 1 (*female*) and 2 (*male*), conduct an independent-samples t test to compare the body temperatures of males and females. Calculate and interpret Cohen's d as a measure of effect size.

4. Using the same worksheet, conduct an independent-samples t test to compare the pulse rates of males and females. Calculate and interpret Cohen's d as a measure of effect size.

6 One-Way ANOVA

Analysis of variance (ANOVA) was developed by statistician R. A. Fisher to test the equality of three or more means. The one-way ANOVA is direct extension of the independent-samples t test to three or more groups. ANOVA partitions or "analyzes" the variation in data into two different sources. Some of the variation is due to differences between the means of the groups. This variation is called **between-groups** variation or treatment effect. Some of the variation is due to differences among the scores within the separate groups. This is called **within-groups** variation or **error** variance. A mean square (MS) is calculated for each source of variation by dividing the sum of squares for the particular source by the appropriate degrees of freedom. In ANOVA, the MSs are the "variances being analyzed." The F ratio used to test the hypothesis of equality among the group means is a ratio of two variance estimates, in this case the MS between divided by the MS within. Like the t distribution, the F distribution is a family of distributions, each defined by the degrees of freedom for the numerator and the degrees of freedom for the denominator.

Excel's Analysis ToolPak provides one-way between-groups analysis ANOVA, one-way within-subjects (repeated measures) ANOVA (as a special case of two-way ANOVA), and two-way ANOVA for a balanced factorial design. The first two cases are covered in this and the next chapter, but this book will not cover two-way ANOVA. You will find that Excel's two-way ANOVA tool is cumbersome and limited, and therefore that for practical purposes you will want to use a dedicated statistics package, an Excel statistics add-in, or regression models with coding variables for more complicated ANOVA designs.

The reader should note that Excel provides no facility for post hoc comparisons after a significant F test, but that it is possible to write simple formulas to perform these tests. Several Excel add-ins provide post hoc or multiple comparisons for means.

Example Data

The following hypothetical data will be used to illustrate the one-way between-groups ANOVA. A statistics professor taught three sections of the same statistics class one semester. One section was taught in a traditional classroom, the second section was an online class that did not meet physically, and the third section was a compressed video class in which students "attended" lectures by the professor that were shown on a large-screen television in their classroom. There were 18 students in each section. All students took the same final examination, and their scores appear in Table 6-1.

Table 6-1. Scores on a statistics final examination

Online	Video	Classroom
56	86	85
75	87	87
59	89	94
88	72	95
68	93	96
63	85	60
90	70	77
63	88	97
60	74	68
53	79	57
97	69	60
53	75	88
53	89	89
70	82	67
79	73	93
90	70	90
75	86	97
98	78	84

The properly formatted data in Excel would appear as shown in Figure 6-1. These data are available from the companion web page.

	A	B	C
1	Online	Video	Classroom
2	56	86	85
3	75	87	87
4	59	89	94
5	88	72	95
6	68	93	96
7	63	85	60
8	90	70	77
9	63	88	97
10	60	74	68
11	53	79	57
12	97	69	60
13	53	75	88
14	53	89	89
15	70	82	67
16	79	73	93
17	90	70	90
18	75	86	97
19	98	78	84
20			

Figure 6-1. Data for one-way ANOVA in Excel

One-Way ANOVA in the Analysis ToolPak

To conduct the one-way ANOVA using the Analysis ToolPak, select **Data >Analysis > Data Analysis**. In the dialog box, select **Anova: Single Factor** and then click **OK**. The ANOVA tool Dialog box appears (see Figure 6-2). Provide the input range including the column labels and click **OK**. If the group sizes are not equal, drag through the entire range to include the group with the largest number of observations, including any blank cells. The resulting descriptive statistics and ANOVA summary table are shown in Figure 6-3.

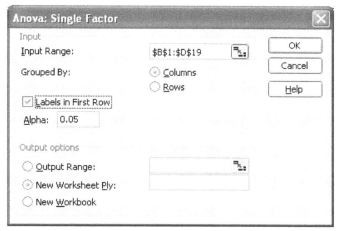

Figure 6-2. One-way ANOVA tool dialog box

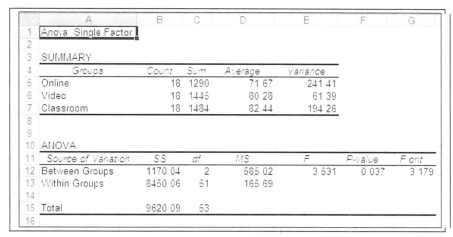

Figure 6-3. Excel's ANOVA summary table

The significant F ratio indicates that there is a difference among the average exam scores for the three sections, $F(2,51) = 3.53$, $p = .037$, $\eta^2 = .12$. Although Excel provides the two-sample F test that you used earlier to check the homogeneity of variance assumption for the independent-samples t test, Excel provides no homogeneity of variance test for three or more groups. SPSS uses the Levene test of homogeneity of variance. The data in the example depart significantly from homogeneity ($p = .011$), thus violating the assumption of homoscedasticity. Additional exploratory analyses reveal that the exam scores depart from normality ($p = .009$). Therefore, it would be better to transform the data or analyze them with a nonparametric test such as the Kruskal-Wallis H test (Thorne & Giesen, 2004). A Kruskal-Wallis test shows that these groups do not have significantly different ranks on the exam scores, $\chi^2(2, N = 54) = 5.00$, $p = .082$. The MegaStat add-in discussed in Appendix D provides the Kruskal-Wallis and other nonparametric tests.

THE BOTTOM LINE
- The one-way ANOVA compares three or more means simultaneously.
- The one-way ANOVA assumes interval or ratio data, independence, normality of distribution, and equality of variance.
- Excel does not provide post hoc comparisons.
- Place data in side-by-side columns with appropriate headings or use named ranges.
- Select **Data > Analysis > Data Analysis > Anova: Single Factor**.

> - Drag through the entire range of data, including the empty cells if the group sizes are not equal.
> - Click **OK** to run the one-way ANOVA.

Effect Size for the One-Way ANOVA

As an effect-size index for the one-way ANOVA, the value η^2 (eta squared) can be calculated very easily by dividing the between-groups sum of squares by the total sum of squares. This value shows the proportion of the variance in the dependent variable that can be explained or accounted for by "treatment" effects or differences among the means. In the current case, even though the F ratio is significant, the value of η^2 is .12, indicating that approximately 12% of the variation in the dependent variable is accounted for by knowledge of the treatment condition. Said differently, the type of class explains a significant but not practically very large proportion of the variation in the statistics exam scores.

Multiple Comparisons in Excel

When you have found a significant F ratio, it is usually of interest to know which means differ from each other. As mentioned earlier, Excel does not provide multiple comparisons, but it is possible to write some rather simple formulas to perform these comparisons.

It usually occurs to the student that he or she could just do an independent-samples t test between each pair of means in the data set. However, doing pairwise t tests increases the likelihood of Type I error (rejecting a true null hypothesis). To see how substantial the compounding of Type I error is, you must first understand the term "experiment-wise error rate." Assume that you are using the conventional standard of .05 as the required level for overall significance for the ANOVA. It is customary to call the probability of Type I error α. As multiple t tests are performed, the probability of rejecting a true null hypothesis quickly surpasses the nominal alpha level. The experiment-wise error rate can be found from the following formula:

$$\alpha_{tot} = 1 - (1 - \alpha_{crit})^c$$

where α_{tot} is the experiment-wise error rate, α_{crit} is the nominal alpha level for each test, and c is the number of tests performed. To illustrate, you just compared three groups. If the alpha level for each of the three pairwise comparisons is set at .05, then the actual experiment-wise error rate would be

$$\alpha_{tot} = 1 - (1 - .05)^3 = 1 - .95^3 = .143$$

Thus, you have more than a .14 probability of rejecting a true null hypothesis when you are performing only three pairwise tests. As the number of tests increases, this probability compounds. For example, with only four groups, there are six possible comparisons, and the experiment-wise error rate for a nominal alpha of .05 for each comparison is .265.

The Fisher LSD Test

Controlling for the experiment-wise error rate is obviously very important. Several approaches have been proposed. R. A. Fisher, the creator of ANOVA, suggested that one perform a "protected t test," in which the overall alpha level for all comparisons is held at α_{crit}. Fisher's test is called LSD for "least significant difference." You can find a critical value of LSD for comparing two group means from the following formula:

$$\text{LSD}_{\alpha} = t_{\alpha}\sqrt{MS_w\left(\frac{1}{n_1} + \frac{1}{n_2}\right)}$$

When group sizes are equal, the value of LSD can be found from this formula:

$$\text{LSD}_{\alpha} = t_{\alpha}\sqrt{\frac{2MS_w}{n}}$$

where $n_1 = n_2 = \ldots = n_k = n$. Because all three groups had 18 observations in the current case, you will need to find only one LSD. If the group sizes are different, different values of LSD must be computed for each comparison. In this equation, α is the chosen alpha level, which is conventionally the same as that for the overall F test, t_{α} is the two-tailed critical value of t for df_w (the within-groups degrees of freedom). MS_w is of course the within-groups mean square, and n is the number of observations in a single sample. Using these values from the ANOVA and the critical value of t found from the T.INV.2T function, you can calculate an LSD for alpha = .05.

$$\text{LSD}_{.05} = 2.00758\sqrt{\frac{2 \times 165.69}{18}} = 8.6139$$

This "least significant difference" is compared to the actual differences among the means. Any difference larger in absolute value than LSD is statistically significant. Building a simple table to display the mean differences (see Table 6-2) makes them easier to compare. Note that this is a two-tailed test and that the sign of the mean difference could be changed simply by reversing the order of subtraction.

Table 6-2. Fisher LSD test of mean differences

	Online	Video	Classroom
Online	-	8.611	10.778*
Video	-	-	2.167
Classroom	-	-	-

*$p < .05$

By the standard of the LSD, only the difference between the classroom and online sections is significant. Note that the comparison between the video classroom and the online section approaches significance.

The Tukey HSD Test

The Fisher LSD is less popular today than the Tukey HSD ("honestly significant difference") and Bonferroni-corrected comparisons. The LSD is too "liberal" for most modern statisticians' tastes. In other words, it is more likely to find significant differences in post hoc comparisons than other more conservative post hoc tests. But the LSD does have the advantage that it makes use of the familiar t distribution, and it also easily accommodates groups of different sizes (Thorne & Giesen, 2004).

The Tukey HSD test uses the "studentized range statistic," a distribution not currently available in Excel. A table of critical values of the studentized range distribution is located in Appendix C, and in many statistics texts. The Tukey HSD test (Tukey, 1949) is somewhat more conservative than the LSD test. This means that a difference between two means will have to be larger to be found significant with the HSD test than with the LSD test. A critical difference can be calculated as:

$$\text{HSD} = q_k \sqrt{\frac{MS_w}{n}}$$

where q is the tabled value of the studentized range statistic with the desired alpha level, k is the total number of treatments or conditions being compared, and n is the number of observations per group. When the sample sizes are not equal, it is customary to calculate the harmonic mean of the sample sizes and use that value, $\tilde{n}$, in place of n when calculating HSD. The harmonic mean of k different sample sizes is

$$\tilde{n} = \frac{k}{1/n_1 + 1/n_2 + \ldots + 1/n_k}$$

Excel has a built-in function for calculating the harmonic mean, HARMEAN. In this case, the samples are of equal size. The HSD for the current comparisons is found as

$$\text{HSD} = q \sqrt{\frac{MS_w}{n}} = 3.418 \sqrt{\frac{165.687}{18}} = 10.370$$

where q is found by interpolation for three means, alpha = .05, and $df_w = 51$ in Appendix C. Note that HSD is larger than LSD, making this a more conservative test, as the discussion indicated it would be. By this criterion as well, the difference between the online and classroom sections is significant.

Bonferroni Corrections

The Bonferroni correction is a simple adjustment to the alpha level to control for the experiment-wise error rate. In general, if you perform k tests and want overall protection at the level of α, then you should use α/k as the criterion for significance for each comparison (Moore, McCabe, Duckworth, & Sclove, 2003). Assuming that the overall alpha level is .05, and that three comparisons are being made, then pairwise t tests can be performed, but the required significance level for each test is $\alpha/3$ or .01667.

Other Post Hoc Tests

As mentioned earlier, statistics packages and some statistics add-ins for Excel include mechanisms for performing post hoc comparisons. For example, SPSS 20 offers 14 choices for post hoc tests assuming equal variances, and an additional four when equal variances are not assumed. In addition to the Fisher LSD, *Introductory Statistics: A Cognitive Learning Approach* (Pace, 2006) shows how to use Excel formulas and functions to conduct Tukey HSD tests, Scheffé tests, and the Dunnett test for multiple comparisons to a control group.

THE BOTTOM LINE
- Excel does not provide multiple comparisons or effect size indices for the one-way ANOVA.

- Eta squared (η^2) is the between-groups sum of squares divided by the total sum of squares, and shows the proportion of the total variation that can be attributed to group differences or treatment effects.
- The Fisher LSD, Tukey HSD, and Bonferroni-corrected comparisons are post hoc tests.
- These post hoc comparisons can be achieved through functions or formulas in Excel.
- Some Excel add-ins provide post hoc comparisons.
- Dedicated statistics packages like SPSS provide many post hoc procedures.

Chapter 6 Exercises

1. Using the data set from Table 2-1, conduct a one-way ANOVA comparing the mean 2001 salaries for the separate regions. Use an alpha level of .05. Build an ANOVA summary table. What is the value of eta squared? If the overall F ratio is significant, conduct a Fisher LSD test or a Tukey HSD test to determine which pairs of means are significantly different at an experiment-wise alpha level of .05. *Hint*: you will find it very helpful to use the Table feature of Excel 2010 to sort and filter the data by region in order to perform the ANOVA. What are your conclusions?

2. Using the same data set, conduct a one-way ANOVA comparing the mean 2001 salaries for the separate regions using the ANOVA tool in the Analysis ToolPak. Use an alpha level of .05. Build an ANOVA summary table. What is the value of eta squared? If the overall F ratio is significant, conduct a Fisher LSD test or a Tukey HSD test to determine which pairs of means are significantly different at an experiment-wise alpha level of .05. What are your conclusions?

3. The fleet manager of a delivery service randomly assigned 15 identical Honda Civics to three groups of five each. Each vehicle was tested at 55 MPH for 400 highway miles. Gasoline mileage was recorded in miles per gallon. The results were as follows:

BrandA	BrandB	BrandC
34.0	35.3	33.3
35.0	36.5	34.0
34.3	36.4	34.7
35.5	37.0	33.0
35.8	37.6	34.9

Enter the data in an Excel workbook file (or download the data from the companion web page). Conduct a one-way ANOVA comparing the mean mileage for the three brands. Use an alpha level of .05. Build an ANOVA summary table. What is the value of eta squared? If the overall F ratio is significant, conduct a Fisher LSD test or a Tukey HSD test to determine which pairs of means are significantly different at an experiment-wise alpha level of .05. Assuming that the gasoline brands are all priced the same, what brand of gasoline should the fleet manager purchase?

4. The fleet manager wants to purchase new compact cars, and finds the following information concerning overall (combined highway and city) gasoline mileage for subcompact cars from different manufacturers (source: http://www.consumerreports.org). Conduct a one-way ANOVA comparing the gasoline mileage of the cars from the five different manufacturers. Use an alpha level of .05. Build an ANOVA summary table. What is the value of eta squared?

If the overall F ratio is significant, conduct a Fisher LSD test or a Tukey HSD test to determine which pairs of means are significantly different at an experiment-wise alpha level of .05. On the basis of your analysis, which manufacturer(s) would you recommend if the goal is to achieve the highest average gasoline mileage?

Honda	Kia	Chevy	Hyundai	Toyota
28	25	24	27	32
37	28	25	27	33
31	28	28	28	34
32	30	27	30	
34				

7 Repeated-Measures ANOVA

The repeated-measures or within-subjects ANOVA is an extension of the paired-samples t test to three or more repeated observations of the same participants or cases. The Analysis ToolPak tool that correctly performs one-way repeated-measures ANOVA is rather awkwardly labeled "Anova: Two-Factor Without Replication." This is because the repeated-measures ANOVA can be considered as a special case of two-way ANOVA with only one observation per cell. The two factors are "subjects" (rows of cases or participants) and "treatments" (the repeated measures). The ANOVA: Two-Factor Without Replication tool produces a summary table in which the subject (row) variable is the within-subjects source of variance, and the columns (conditions) factor is the between-groups source of variance.

In general, the repeated-measures ANOVA is more powerful statistically than the between-groups ANOVA because individual differences are controlled statistically by allocating them to systematic variance. The error term is thus reduced, and the resulting test is more sensitive. This increased power often comes with a price tag. Research designs making use of repeated measures are sensitive to such subject variables as learning, order effects, practice, and fatigue, whereas these variables are more readily controlled in the between-groups designs by random assignment to conditions. In repeated-measures designs, such factors can often be addressed through counterbalancing.

The repeated-measures ANOVA assumes that the data are interval or ratio in nature, that the sample is randomly selected from a population of normally-distributed observations, that the observations within the sample are independent, that the population variances of the treatments or conditions are equal, and finally that the population covariances for all pairs of treatments are equal.

Example Data

Twelve students participated in a "mental rotation" task. A stimulus figure was presented and then either the same or a different (mirror-image) figure was presented rotated at 45, 90, 135, 180, 225, 270, or 315 degrees. Participants determined whether the rotated figure was the same or different from the stimulus figure. To control for order effects, the computer randomized the presentation of the rotated figures. The dependent variable was the number of correct identifications a student made from the three matching figures for each angle. The data are available at the companion web page and are presented in Table 7-1.

Table 7-1. Example data for repeated-measures ANOVA

Student	ANG45	ANG90	ANG135	ANG180	ANG225	ANG270	ANG315
1	3	2	2	2	1	2	3
2	3	1	0	3	2	3	3
3	2	3	3	2	3	3	3
4	2	3	3	3	2	3	3
5	3	3	2	0	3	3	2
6	3	3	2	2	2	2	3
7	3	3	2	2	3	3	3
8	2	1	2	1	2	1	3
9	3	3	1	3	2	0	2
10	3	3	3	3	3	3	3
11	3	3	3	3	3	3	3
12	3	2	0	0	1	1	2

The properly configured data in Excel appear as follows (see Figure 7-1). When you use Excel for repeated measures, it is helpful to include the case or participant number.

	A	B	C	D	E	F	G	H
1	Student	ANG45	ANG90	ANG135	ANG180	ANG225	ANG270	ANG315
2	1	3	2	2	2	1	2	3
3	2	3	1	0	3	2	3	3
4	3	2	3	3	2	3	3	3
5	4	2	3	3	3	2	3	3
6	5	3	3	2	0	3	3	2
7	6	3	3	2	2	2	2	3
8	7	3	3	2	2	3	3	3
9	8	2	1	2	1	2	1	3
10	9	3	3	1	3	2	0	2
11	10	3	3	3	3	3	3	3
12	11	3	3	3	3	3	3	3
13	12	3	2	0	0	1	1	2
14								

Figure 7-1. Excel data for repeated-measures ANOVA

Repeated-measures ANOVA in the Analysis ToolPak

To conduct the repeated-measures ANOVA, use the "Anova: Two-Factor Without Replication tool" in the Analysis ToolPak, as shown in Figure 7-2. Include the row of data labels, make sure that you check the box in front of "Labels," and also be sure to include the column of student numbers in the input range. It is the "rows" variable. If you are not using labels, then you should omit the student numbers along with the row of data labels.

The output is placed by default in a new worksheet, or optionally in the same worksheet with the data. The ANOVA summary table formatted and then copied from Excel appears in Table 7-2.

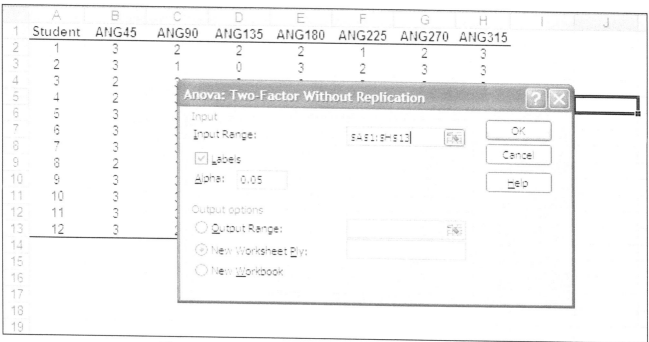

Figure 7-2. Using Excel for Repeated-measures ANOVA.

Table 7-2. Summary output from repeated-measures ANOVA

ANOVA

Source of Variation	SS	df	MS	F	P-value	F crit
Rows	20.988	11	1.908	3.505	0.001	1.937
Columns	8.071	6	1.345	2.471	0.032	2.239
Error	35.929	66	0.544			
Total	64.988	83				

The test of interest is the F ratio for "Columns," the treatment comparison. It is typically of less interest to know whether the within-subjects or "Rows" F ratio is significant. This test is telling you what you probably already know—that different individuals have differing levels of mental rotation skill. The angle of rotation makes a difference in the correct identification of the matching figures, $F(6,66) = 2.47$, $p = .032$.

THE BOTTOM LINE

- The repeated-measures ANOVA allocates individual differences to systematic error and is generally more powerful than the between-groups ANOVA.
- Repeated-measures designs are sensitive to learning, order effects, practice, and fatigue. These factors can often be addressed through counterbalancing.
- The tool in Excel that performs repeated-measures ANOVA is labeled "Anova: Two-Factor Without Replication."
- To access this tool, select Data > Analysis > Data Analysis > Anova: Two-Factor Without Replication.
- The F ratio of interest is the "columns" or treatment comparison.

Multiple Comparisons in the Repeated-Measures ANOVA

As with the one-way ANOVA, Excel provides no follow-up or post hoc comparisons for the repeated-measures ANOVA. However, you can make a simple adjustment to the Fisher LSD or Tukey HSD tests introduced in the previous chapter and use that adjustment as the basis for multiple comparisons in the repeated-measures ANOVA.

The only minor adjustment for LSD or HSD with the repeated-measures ANOVA is that one uses MS_{error} and df_{error} rather than MS_w and df_w (Thorne & Giesen, 2003). Otherwise all calculations are identical to those shown earlier. Because there are repeated measures on the same individuals or cases, you will need only one value for LSD. Calculate modified LSD for an alpha level of .05. You can easily find the two-tailed critical value of t for $\alpha = .05$ and 66 df by using the TINV function:

$$=\text{T.INV}(.05,\ 66) = 1.9966$$

By use of the previous formula, you calculate LSD$_{.05}$ to be

$$LSD = t_\alpha \sqrt{\frac{2MS_{error}}{n}} = 1.9966\sqrt{\frac{2\times.5443}{12}} = .601$$

Similarly, you can find Tukey's HSD criterion:

$$HSD = q\sqrt{\frac{MS_{error}}{n}} = 4.15\sqrt{\frac{.5443}{12}} = .88$$

The value of q was found by interpolation in Appendix C. As with the one-way ANOVA, you can report the post hoc comparisons with a table of mean differences using the LSD or the HSD test as follows (see Table 7-3). The LSD test produced significant comparisons for 45 degrees compared to 135 and 180 degrees, for 135 degrees compared to 315 degrees, and for 180 degrees compared to 315. None of the differences are significant by the HSD criterion, though the comparisons for 45 and 135 and 135 and 315 approach significance.

Table 7-3. Post hoc comparisons for repeated-measures ANOVA (LSD test)

	ANG45	ANG90	ANG135	ANG180	ANG225	ANG270	ANG315
ANG45	-	0.250	0.833*	0.75*	0.500	0.500	0.000
ANG90	-	-	0.583	0.500	0.250	0.250	-0.250
ANG135	-	-	-	-0.083	-0.333	-0.333	-0.833*
ANG180	-	-	-	-	-0.250	-0.250	-0.75*
ANG225	-	-	-	-	-	0.000	-0.500
ANG270	-	-	-	-	-	-	-0.500
ANG315	-	-	-	-	-	-	-

*$p < .05$ (LSD)

A means plot can be used for a visual inspection of these differences (see Figure 7-3).

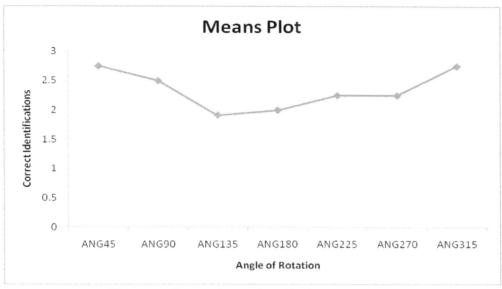

Figure 7-3. Means plot produced by Line Graph tool

The means plot makes it clear that rotations closer to the original stimulus figure tend to produce a higher number of correct identifications, while more extreme rotations tend to produce a lower number of correct identifications.

Effect Size in Repeated-Measures ANOVA

For the repeated-measures ANOVA, a "partial eta squared" can be calculated by dividing $SS_{columns}$ by the $SS_{columns} + SS_{error}$. In this case, $\eta_p^2 = 8.071/(8.071 + 35.929) = .18$. A worksheet template (not shown) for conducting the repeated-measures ANOVA is available at the companion web page. The template conducts the repeated-measures ANOVA for up to ten repeated measures and calculates the value of partial eta squared as well as the LSD criterion for mean comparisons.

THE BOTTOM LINE
- Excel provides no facility for post hoc comparisons in the repeated-measures ANOVA.
- LSD and HSD comparisons can be made by using MS_{error} and df_{error} rather than MS_w and df_w.
- Partial eta squared is an appropriate effect-size index for the repeated-measures ANOVA.
- Partial eta squared can be calculated as $SS_{columns} / (SS_{columns} + SS_{error})$.

Chapter 7 Exercises

1. The following scores represent job competency scores on a scale of 0 (*incompetent*) to 10 (*fully competent*) of 10 workers before a training program, immediately after the program, 3 months after the program, and 6 months after the program. Conduct a repeated-measures ANOVA. If the overall F ratio for "columns" is significant, conduct a post hoc analysis using the modified Fisher LSD test or the modified Tukey HSD test. Did the training program appear to be effective?

Worker	Before	After	3Mo	6Mo
1	6	8	10	10
2	0	4	5	6
3	2	4	6	8
4	6	7	9	9
5	6	5	6	8
6	3	4	8	7
7	6	9	10	9
8	0	2	3	4
9	1	2	6	6
10	0	1	3	5

2. The following data represent customer quality ratings on a scale of 1 (*poor*) to 5 (*excellent*) for 7 l of a national hotel chain in a given city. The ratings are collected every month. Conduct a repeated-measures ANOVA. If the overall F ratio for "columns" is significant, conduct a post hoc analysis using the modified Fisher LSD test or the modified Tukey HSD test. Is quality improving?

Location	Mo1	Mo2	Mo3	Mo4
1	3	3	5	5
2	1	4	3	4
3	1	2	4	5
4	2	3	3	3
5	3	4	5	5
6	3	3	3	4
7	2	5	3	5

3. The following data represent the ratings of six different products by four different judges. Do the judges rate the products similarly? In this case, an insignificant "columns" F ratio would indicate agreement among the judges. Conduct a repeated-measures ANOVA. If the overall F ratio for "columns" is significant, conduct a post hoc analysis using the modified Fisher LSD test or the modified Tukey HSD test. What do you conclude?

Product	Judge1	Judge2	Judge3	Judge4
1	2	4	3	3
2	5	7	5	6
3	1	3	1	2
4	7	9	9	8
5	2	4	6	1
6	6	8	8	4

4. The following data were provided by J.D. Power and Associates concerning the North American Guest Satisfaction Index for eight midscale full-service hotel chains for the years 2004 – 2006. Is hotel quality improving? Conduct a repeated-measures ANOVA. If the overall F ratio for "columns" is significant, conduct a post hoc analysis using the modified Fisher LSD test or the modified Tukey HSD test. What do you conclude?

Chain	2004	2005	2006
1	779	807	804
2	722	721	743
3	714	689	722
4	769	782	791
5	733	720	750
6	686	678	685
7	704	713	732
8	672	696	712

8 Correlation and Regression

This brief text addresses only the bivariate (two variables) case of correlation and regression. There is a *predictor* or independent variable x and a *criterion* or dependent variable y. You are interested in examining the linear relationship between the two variables and determining the equation for a line of best fit for predicting y from x. Each case has a measurement for both x and y. We calculate the correlation between x and y by dividing the covariance of x and y by the product of the standard deviations of x and y:

$$r_{xy} = \frac{s_{xy}}{s_x s_y}$$

Excel has several useful functions for correlation and regression. Simply to find the Pearson product-moment correlation between the two variables, you may use the built-in function CORREL(Array1, Array2) where Array1 and Array2 are the ranges for the x and y variables. The regression coefficient (slope) for a bivariate correlation can be found by the function SLOPE(Array Y, Array X) where Array Y is the range of observed y values and Array X is the range of observed x values. The intercept term can be found by use of the function INTERCEPT(Array Y, Array X) where the two arrays are defined as above. To determine a predicted value of y for a given value of x, you can enter the function FORECAST(X, Array Y, Array X) and replace x with the value for which you want to predict the value of y.

You can also derive an intercorrelation matrix for two or more variables by using the Correlation tool in the Analysis ToolPak. The Regression tool in the Analysis ToolPak supplies the value of the correlation, regression, and intercept coefficients, and also performs an analysis of variance of the significance of the regression. Excel's Regression tool performs both simple and multiple regression analyses. This chapter illustrates simple linear regression.

Example Data

For convenience, the data used to illustrate the scatterplot in Chapter 3 (Table 3-2, page 82) are repeated in Table 8-1 and are also available at the companion web page. You will first learn the built-in functions for correlation, slope, intercept, and prediction. Then, you will learn to perform a complete regression analysis using the Analysis ToolPak.

Table 8-1. Study hours and GPA

Student	Hours	GPA	Student	Hours	GPA
1	10	3.33	11	13	3.26
2	12	2.92	12	12	3.00
3	10	2.56	13	11	2.74
4	15	3.08	14	10	2.85
5	14	3.57	15	13	3.33
6	12	3.31	16	13	3.29
7	13	3.45	17	14	3.58
8	15	3.93	18	18	3.85
9	16	3.82	19	17	4.00
10	14	3.70	20	14	3.50

If you are building your worksheet, place the data in an Excel workbook as shown in Figure 8-1.

	A	B	C
1	Student	Hours	GPA
2	1	10	3.33
3	2	12	2.92
4	3	10	2.56
5	4	15	3.08
6	5	14	3.57
7	6	12	3.31
8	7	13	3.45
9	8	15	3.93
10	9	16	3.82
11	10	14	3.70
12	11	13	3.26
13	12	12	3.00
14	13	11	2.74
15	14	10	2.85
16	15	13	3.33
17	16	13	3.29
18	17	14	3.58
19	18	18	3.85
20	19	17	4.00
21	20	14	3.50

Figure 8-1. Excel data for regression analysis

Correlation, Slope, Intercept, and Forecasting

For convenience, name the hours and GPA variable ranges. If you need a refresher, named ranges are discussed in Chapter 1. These named ranges make Excel formulas and functions easier to understand and explain to others. You can use Excel to find the value of the Pearson product moment correlation, and also to calculate the regression equation

$$\hat{y} = b_0 + b_1 x$$

Where b_0 is the y-intercept term and b_1 is the slope or regression coefficient. The regression coefficient b_1 can be calculated from the correlation and the standard deviations of x and y:

$$b_1 = r_{xy}\left(\frac{s_y}{s_x}\right)$$

The y-intercept term can be calculated as follows:

$$b_0 = \bar{y} - b_1 \bar{x}$$

Figure 8-2 displays the Formula View of the use of the functions for the correlation, intercept, and slope terms. Next, you can see the Value View to show the results (Figure 8-3). Note that the order of the variables does not affect the value of the correlation coefficient, but it does affect the values of the slope and intercept. You are "regressing" the criterion y (GPA) onto the predictor x (study hours). Notice that the CORREL, SLOPE, and INTERCEPT terms are calculated and reported by their relevant functions, but there is no test for statistical significance.

Enter the CORREL function by going to the blank cell where you want the result to display, and then type

$$=CORREL(Array1, Array2)$$

If you have named the ranges, then just type the names of the ranges in your formula. For the CORREL function, it is immaterial whether you place the x array first or the y array first, because $r_{xy} = r_{yx}$. However, it is important that you get the arrays in the right order for the SLOPE and INTERCEPT functions. For these functions, the y array must come before the x array. If you accidentally enter the x array first, it will be treated as the criterion variable, and you will be regressing x onto y, which although possible mathematically, is not what you want to do in this case.

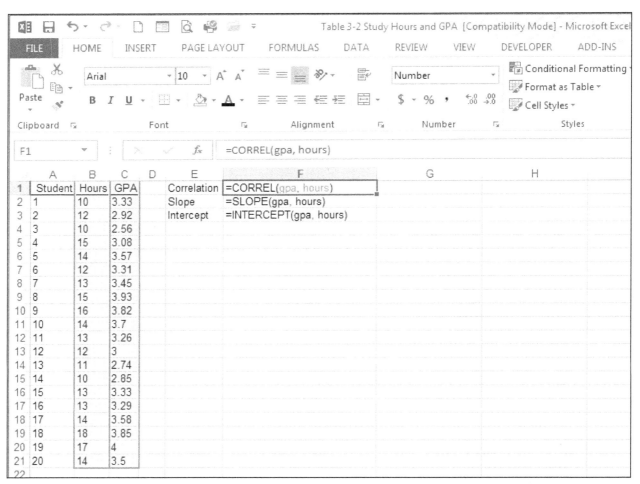

Figure 8-2. Using Excel functions for correlation, slope, and intercept terms (Formula View)

	A	B	C	D	E	F	G
1	Student	Hours	GPA		Correlation	0.817	
2	1	10	3.33		Slope	0.149	
3	2	12	2.92		Intercept	1.373	
4	3	10	2.56				
5	4	15	3.08				
6	5	14	3.57				
7	6	12	3.31				

Figure 8-3. Value View of correlation, slope, and intercept

The slope and intercept define the equation of the line of best fit for the observed values of y and x. This is the linear regression equation for predicting a student's GPA based on knowledge of that student's study hours. In the current case, the equation is:

$$\hat{y} = b_0 + b_1 x = 1.373 + 0.149 \times \text{hours}$$

Assuming that the regression coefficient is statistically significant, this equation can be used to predict a GPA for any value of study hours, even those not observed in the sample. For example, to predict the GPA of a student who studies 8 hours per week, the equation would produce the following result:

$$\hat{y} = 1.373 + 0.149 \times 8 = 2.56$$

Excel has a built-in function called FORECAST that can instantly produce this value, and the predicted value for any particular value of x. To use this function, one supplies the desired value of x, and the "known" or observed ranges of x and y as shown in Figure 8-4. Examine in Figure 8-4 the FORECAST function displayed in the Formula Bar. We return briefly to forecasting at the end of this chapter, but first, you will learn more about using the Regression tool in Excel.

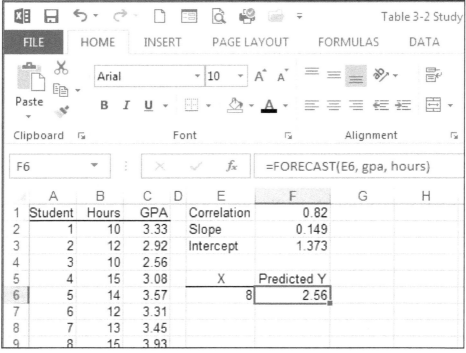

Figure 8-4. Using the FORECAST function

THE BOTTOM LINE

- The correlation between two variables can be found by use of the CORREL function, =CORREL(Array1, Array2) where Array1 and Array2 are the *x* and *y* variables. The order of entry of *x* and *y* is immaterial with correlation. The significance of the correlation coefficient is not tested.
- The slope of the line of best fit is found by use of the SLOPE function, =SLOPE(ArrayY, ArrayX) where *y* is the criterion variable and *x* is the predictor. The order of entry of the arrays is important for the correct slope to display.
- The *y*-intercept is found by use of the INTERCEPT function, =INTERCEPT(ArrayY, ArrayX). The order of entry is important for the correct intercept to display.
- The FORECAST function can be used to predict a value of *y* for any value of *x* by use of the linear regression equation.

Regression Analysis in the Analysis ToolPak

The Regression tool in the Analysis ToolPak reports the correlation coefficient, the slope, and the intercept, and performs a significance test on the overall regression, along with an equivalent test of the significance of the regression (slope) coefficient. The same tool is used for multiple regression with two or more predictors and a single criterion. Therefore, the value of r_{xy} will be called "Multiple R." This value will always be zero or positive, but if the original correlation r_{xy} is negative, the slope term will be negative. To perform a regression analysis, select **Data > Analysis > Data Analysis > Regression** (see Figure 8-5).

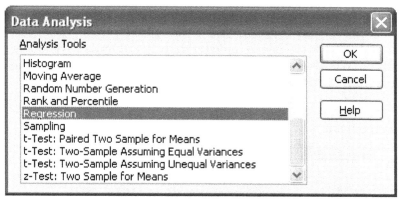

Figure 8-5. Selecting the Regression tool

Click **OK**. The Regression dialog appears (see Figure 8-6).

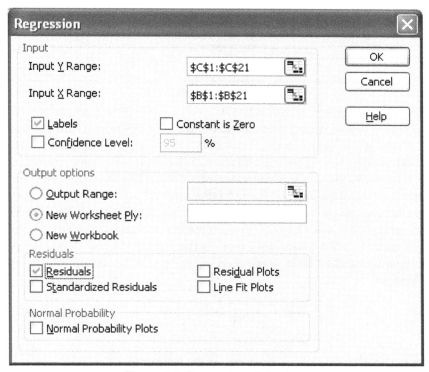

Figure 8-6. Regression dialog box

Enter the range of cell references or the named range for the y variable (GPA) including the column heading. You can drag through the range or type in the cell references. Enter the range for the x variable in the same way. Check the box to indicate that the columns have labels in the first row. In this case you have also asked for residuals and accepted the default to place the output in a new worksheet (see Figure 8-6). The Regression tool output is shown in Table 8-2.

Table 8-2. Regression tool output

SUMMARY OUTPUT

Regression Statistics	
Multiple R	0.817
R Square	0.668
Adjusted R Square	0.650
Standard Error	0.240
Observations	20

ANOVA

	df	SS	MS	F	Significance F
Regression	1	2.089	2.089	36.261	0.000
Residual	18	1.037	0.058		
Total	19	3.126			

	Coefficients	Standard Error	t Stat	P-value	Lower 95%	Upper 95%
Intercept	1.373	0.333	4.119	0.001	0.673	2.073
Hours	0.149	0.025	6.022	0.000	0.097	0.201

The value "Multiple R" is the correlation between y and $\hat{y}$ (and also the absolute value of the Pearson product-moment correlation between GPA and study hours you found earlier). In the two-variable case, the F test of the significance of the linear regression is mathematically and statistically identical to the t-test of the significance of the regression coefficient for study hours. The square root of the F ratio, 36.261, equals the value of t, 6.022. The statistically significant regression indicates that study hours can be used to predict GPA, and R^2 indicates that roughly 67 percent of the variation in grades can be explained by knowing one's study hours. Note that R^2 can also be calculated by dividing the $SS_{\text{regression}}$ by the SS_{total}. This is the "correlation ratio," or eta squared in ANOVA terms. The value labeled "standard error" is the standard error of estimate, a measure of the accuracy of predictions using the linear regression equation. For sample data, the standard error of estimate is calculated as:

$$s_{est} = \sqrt{\frac{\sum (y - \hat{y})^2}{n - 2}}$$

Adjusted R-square is the estimate of the population R^2, taking into account both the sample size and the number of predictors. Though the calculated R^2 can never be negative, the adjusted value can be, when the sample value is very close to zero, or when the number of predictors is large relative to the number of observations.

The regression equation $\hat{y} = b_0 + b_1 x$ can be determined from the output from the Regression tool output to be $\hat{y} = 1.373 + 0.149 \times hours$, as discussed previously. A residual can be calculated by subtracting the predicted value of x from the observed value. The optional residual output (see Table 8-3) appears below the summary output.

Table 8-3. Optional residual output from the Regression tool

RESIDUAL OUTPUT

Observation	Predicted GPA	Residuals
1	2.862	0.468
2	3.160	-0.240
3	2.862	-0.302
4	3.607	-0.527
5	3.458	0.112
6	3.160	0.150
7	3.309	0.141
8	3.607	0.323
9	3.756	0.064
10	3.458	0.242
11	3.309	-0.049
12	3.160	-0.160
13	3.011	-0.271
14	2.862	-0.012
15	3.309	0.021
16	3.309	-0.019
17	3.458	0.122
18	4.053	-0.203
19	3.905	0.095
20	3.458	0.042

THE BOTTOM LINE
- The Regression tool in the Analysis ToolPak performs a complete regression analysis for one criterion and one or more predictors.
- To access this tool, select **Data > Analysis > Data Analysis > Regression**.
- The Regression tool conducts an analysis of variance of the overall regression and calculates various summary statistics.
- This tool calculates the slope and intercept terms, and tests the significance of these terms.
- The Regression tool optionally produces residuals and residual plots.

A Brief Introduction to Time Series and Forecasting

Now that you know how to use the Regression tool, let us revisit forecasting and briefly discuss time series data. In many cases, you are interested in the changes in a dependent or criterion variable over time. Measures of a variable taken at regular intervals over time are called a time series (Moore, McCabe, Duckworth, & Sclove, 2003). In such cases the predictor or x variable is successive time periods—or more often an index variable based on these time periods. If the relationship between time and changes in the dependent variable plots a line or something resembling a straight line, then linear regression and forecasting can be used to model the relationship and to predict future values of the dependent variable.

In other cases, the relationship may not be linear, but it might still be monotonic decreasing or increasing in a curvilinear fashion. In such cases, a simple transformation of the data may often result in the ability to use linear regression with the transformed variables.

This book presents only two simple cases, but interested readers are referred to an econometrics text for other extensions to the regression model for dealing with violations of the classical assumptions of regression as well as for coverage of more sophisticated regression-based models. The common problems to be dealt with in regression generally and time series analysis in particular are autocorrelation (or serial correlation), multicollinearity, and heteroscedasticity. A good basic econometrics text such as Studenmund (2006) discusses these problems and methods for dealing with them. Two examples are discussed below, one for which a linear model appears to be appropriate, one in which an exponential model appears more effective. Advanced techniques provide "smoothing" and "deseasonalizing" methods for dealing with time series data that have regular seasonal or cyclical patterns. If a straight line fits the observed data well, one may use linear forecasting, a direct extension of regression to time series data. If a curved line fits the data well, it is often possible to use models that take the curvature of the line into account via data transformations.

To reiterate, a time series is a set of multiple observations of the same variable or variables over a period of time: daily, weekly, monthly, quarterly, or yearly. An example is the annual fall enrollment for a college or university. Another example is a bank's monthly deposits for a period of several years. An analysis of time series data can help you understand the current situation as well as make informed predictions—forecasts—about the future state of affairs.

A time series can have four different components (Lind, Marchal, & Wathen, 2007). These are the trend, the cyclical variation, the seasonal variation, and the irregular variation. This book only considers the trend and irregular variation. In the analyses below, the irregular variation will be attributed to error, and the trend will be found either to be linear or curvilinear.

Linear Trend

The trend (sometimes called the *secular trend*) is the smooth long-term direction of a time series. Consider for example the following data (See Table 8-4), which show the per capita personal income of South Carolina residents from the years 1990 to 2006. These data were obtained from the Bureau of Economic Analysis and are available at the companion web page:

Table 8-4. South Carolina per capita income, 1990 – 2006

Year	Income
1990	15894
1991	16241
1992	16953
1993	17531
1994	18365
1995	19124
1996	20058
1997	20987
1998	22161
1999	23075
2000	24423
2001	24974
2002	25348
2003	25852
2004	27039
2005	28460
2006	29767

A time series plot of these data (see Figure 8-7) shows a relatively smooth and steady increase in personal income over the years, and a linear model would appear to be appropriate for describing the trend. You can fit a line to the observed data points using linear regression. By formatting the data with a trend line using the Scatterplot tool discussed in Chapter 3, you can also display the equation for the line of best fit and the value of r^2 on the scatterplot (see Figure 8-8). In this case, the x variable is the year of the observation, or an index number representing the years in order, and y is the per capita income.

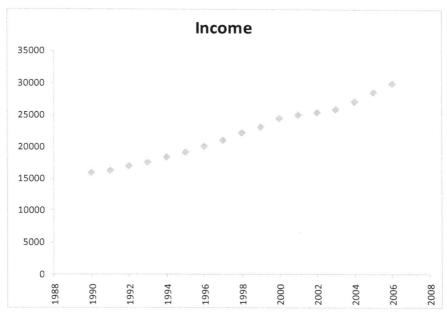

Figure 8-7. The relationship appears to be linear

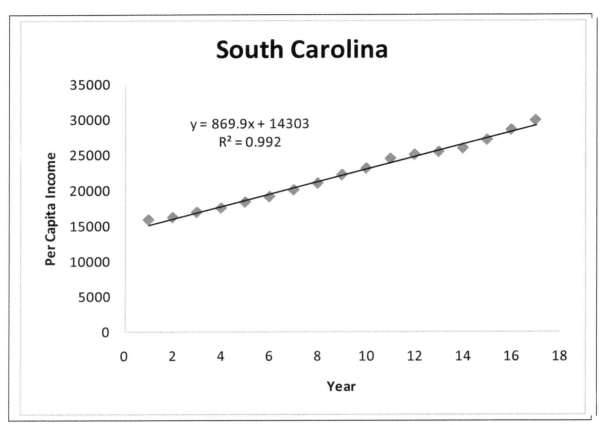

Figure 8-8. Adding a trend line and the regression equation

To test the significance of the regression, you will use the Regression tool. The output is displayed in Table 8-5.

Table 8-5. Regression analysis of income data

SUMMARY OUTPUT

Regression Statistics	
Multiple R	0.9960
R Square	0.9920
Adjusted R Square	0.9915
Standard Error	407.7536
Observations	17

ANOVA

	df	SS	MS	F	Significance F
Regression	1	308,776,921.1863	308,776,921.1863	1,857.1595	0.0000
Residual	15	2,493,945.0490	166,263.0033		
Total	16	311,270,866.2353			

	Coefficients	Standard Error	t Stat	P-value	Lower 95%	Upper 95%
Intercept	14,302.9559	206.8533	69.1454	0.0000	13,862.0586	14,743.8532
Index	869.9461	20.1868	43.0948	0.0000	826.9189	912.9732

After verifying that the regression is significant, you can now use the slope and intercept terms to predict the per capita incomes for subsequent years. This is simplified by Excel's built-in FORECAST function discussed earlier (see Table 8-6).

Table 8-6. Forecasts for 2007–2010

Year	Index	Forecast
2007	18	29961.99
2008	19	30958.12
2009	20	31882.89
2010	21	32819.89

These projections were fairly accurate, as the actual numbers reported by the government for these years were $31990, $32971, $31448, and $32193, respectively.

Nonlinear Trend

Consider the following hypothetical annual sales data (in $000s) for a growing business over the years 1998–2012 (see Table 8-7).

Table 8-7. Hypothetical sales figures for a growing business

Year	Sales
1998	124.2
1999	175.6
2000	306.9
2001	524.2
2002	714.0
2003	1052.0
2004	1638.3
2005	2463.2
2006	3358.2
2007	4181.3
2008	5388.5
2009	8027.4
2010	10587.4
2011	13537.4
2012	17515.6

Plotting the time series indicates that a straight line would be a poor fit to these data. However, a smooth curved line would appear to fit the data well (see Figure 8-9).

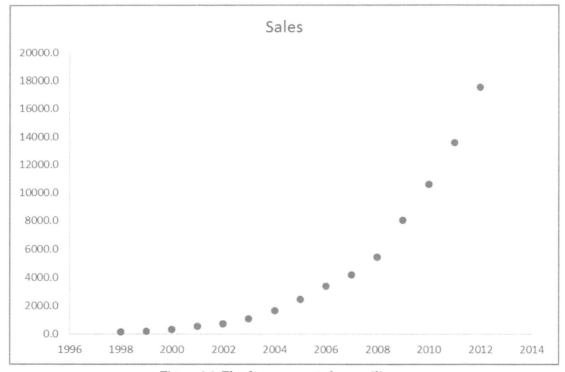

Figure 8-9. The data appear to be curvilinear

Such data can easily be accommodated in a trend analysis by the use of a logarithmic transformation. You will simply find the base 10 logarithm of each year's data and then use the logarithms as the dependent variable and the year (or the coded index number) as the independent variable. To transform a variable to a base 10 logarithm, use the following Excel function:

$$\texttt{=LOG10(Y)}$$

substituting the raw sales for y. Now, a linear regression equation using the ordinary least squares method can be used to determine the model fit. Note that although a straight line clearly does not fit the original observations, the log sales are rather well described by a linear model (see Figure 8-10).

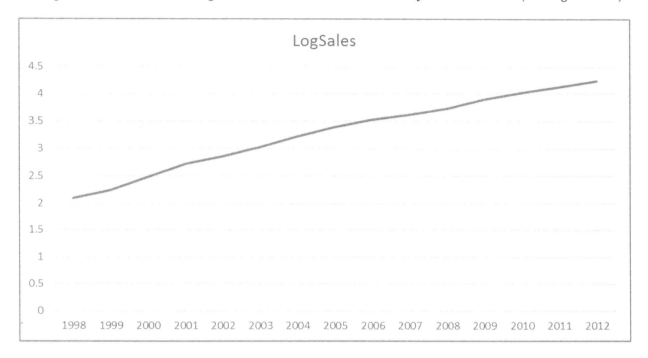

Figure 8-10. The log transformation produces a linear relationship

The regression analysis of the log-transformed sales data appears as follows (see Table 8-8).

Table 8-8. Regression analysis for log-transformed data

SUMMARY OUTPUT

Regression Statistics	
Multiple R	0.993953309
R Square	0.98794318
Adjusted R Square	0.987015732
Standard Error	0.078625262
Observations	15

ANOVA

	df	SS	MS	F	Significance F
Regression	1	6.585166291	6.585166291	1065.2279	7.3607E-14
Residual	13	0.080365114	0.006181932		
Total	14	6.665531405			

	Coefficients	Standard Error	t Stat	P-value	Lower 95%	Upper 95%
Intercept	2.053805148	0.042721678	48.0740747	4.98466E-16	1.961510574	2.146099723
Index	0.153357266	0.004698758	32.63782928	7.3607E-14	0.143206216	0.163508316

Clearly the log-transformed data are linear over time. Using the FORECAST function, we can forecast the estimated log sales for future years by use of the regression equation, and then find the "antilog" of the estimated log sales for that year (see Figure 8-11) to convert the logarithm back to dollars. Remember that you used base 10 logarithms, so the forecasted sales are simply found by taking 10 to the power of the estimated log sales for a given year. As you will recall from an earlier chapter, one performs exponentiation in Excel by using the caret symbol (^) as shown in the Formula Bar in Figure 8-11).

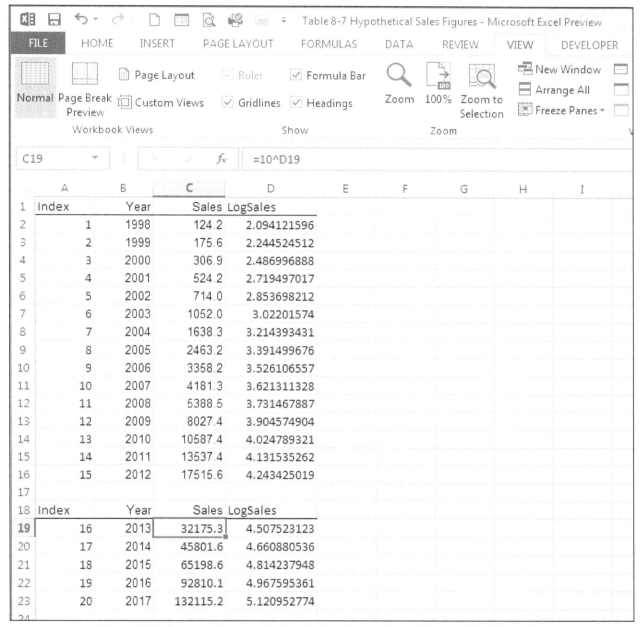

Figure 8-11. Forecast future sales by finding the antilog of the predicted log sales

---

THE BOTTOM LINE

- Time series data are repeated observations over regular time periods.
- Time series data that show a linear trend can be analyzed directly by using the time period or an index number as the predictor.
- Time series data that show a curvilinear trend can often be transformed by logarithmic transformations to allow the use of regression models.
- Advanced time-series analyses are beyond the scope of this text.

Chapter 8 Exercises

1. Using the data from Exercise 3.5, calculate the correlation between 2007 unemployment rate and 2007 weekly wage for the eight educational attainment groups. Determine the regression coefficient (slope) and intercept term for the line of best fit. Test the significance of the correlation. Note: use unemployment rate as the y variable and weekly wage as the x variable. What can you conclude?

2. Using the data from Table 2-1, calculate the correlation between 2001 wages and 2002 wages. Determine the regression coefficient (slope) and intercept term for the line of best fit. Test the significance of the correlation. Note: use 2002 wages as the y variable and 2001 wages as the x variable. What can you conclude?

3. The following data show the annual sales of JC Penney for the years 2003 to 2007 (source: www.jcpenney.net):

Year	Sales($Millions)
2003	17513
2004	18096
2005	18781
2006	19903
2007	19860

   Develop a time series plot of these data and fit a trend line. Conduct a regression analysis of these sales. Test the significance of the correlation. If the overall correlation is significant, use your regression equation, forecast sales for 2008 – 2010.

4. Calculate the correlation between the Time1 and Time2 scores for the data in Table 5-5. Determine the regression coefficient (slope) and intercept term for the line of best fit. Note: use Time2 as the y variable and Time1 as the x variable.

9 Chi-Square Tests

Like the product-moment correlation coefficient, the chi-square distribution was a contribution of statistician Karl Pearson. In this text, chi-square tests are used to compare observed frequencies in the categories of one or two qualitative variables to the frequencies expected if the null hypothesis is true. This chapter covers both one-way (goodness-of-fit) tests and two-way tests of independence. The chi-square distribution has many other uses besides the ones discussed here.

Excel does not directly calculate the value of chi square for either the test of goodness of fit or the test of independence, but it has several built-in chi-square functions. These functions include

- ☐ CHISQ.INV—this is the "inverse" of the chi-square distribution, and will return a value of chi square for a given degrees of freedom and probability level. [2]
- ☐ CHISQ.INV.RT—this function returns the inverse of the right-tailed probability of the chi-square distribution.
- ☐ CHISQ.DIST—this function returns the left-tailed probability of the chi-square distribution. The usage is CHISQ.DIST(chi-square, deg_freedom, CUMULATIVE). CUMULATIVE is either TRUE for the cumulative chi-square distribution, or FALSE for the probability density function.
- ☐ CHISQ.DIST.RT—this function returns the right-tailed probability of the chi-square distribution.
- ☐ CHISQ.TEST—This function requires an array of observed and an array of expected frequencies, and returns the p value of a chi-square test of goodness of fit or a chi-square test of independence. It reports the probability (p value) of the chi-square test result, but not the computed sample value of chi square.

For compatibility's sake, here are the legacy chi-square functions that still work in Excel 2010, but are replaced by the newer functions:

- ☐ CHIINV—the inverse of the chi-square distribution.
- ☐ CHIDIST—the left-tailed probability of the chi-square distribution.
- ☐ CHITEST—the p value for a test of goodness of fit or a test of independence.
- ☐

To use the CHISQ.TEST tool, you must input the observed frequencies and the frequencies expected under the null hypothesis. After you find the p level from the CHISQ.TEST tool, you could use that value and the degrees of freedom to determine the computed value of chi-square by use of the CHISQ.INV function with the proviso noted in the footnote.

---

[2] The previous chi-square function algorithms in Excel did not calculate correct values for the extremes ($p < .0000003$) of the chi-square distribution or for very large degrees of freedom. In such cases, the CHIINV function returns a #NUM error. The only currently useful application of CHIINV is to find critical values. Fortunately, the new CHISQ.INV, CHISQ.INV.RT, CHISQ.TEST and CHISQ.DIST, and CHISQ.DIST.RT functions continue to work correctly in the extreme tails of the distribution.

Chi-Square Goodness-of-Fit Tests

The chi-square goodness-of-fit test compares an array of observed frequencies for levels of a single variable with the associated array of expected frequencies under some null hypothesis. The data may be nominal, or they may be grouped frequencies for a test of the fit of observed cases to a theoretical model such as the normal or some other continuous distribution. The null hypothesis may state that the expected frequencies are uniformly distributed across the levels of the variable, or that they follow a theoretical distribution of values. Thus the chi-square goodness-of-fit test can be used as an convenient alternative to Kolmogorov-Smirnov and Anderson-Darling tests. Unlike those tests, however, chi-square tests can also be applied to discrete distributions like the binomial or the Poisson distributions, making chi-square tests a very flexible tool.

Chi-Square Test of Goodness of Fit for Equal Expected Frequencies

Table 9-1 presents hypothetical data concerning the reasons consumers switch brands even when they report an initial high level of satisfaction with their brand of choice. Two hundred customers were surveyed, and were asked to identify their most important reason for switching brands. To make the categories mutually exclusive and collectively exhaustive, a category called "other" was added to the survey. Assume that the reasons were distributed as follows:

Table 9-1. Reasons for switching brands (hypothetical data)

Reason for Switching Brands	Frequency
Preferred Brand Not Available	32
Less Expensive Alternative	17
New Brand Available	16
Dissatisfied with Current Brand	37
Just Looking for a Change	33
Negative Publicity about Current Brand	35
Positive Promotion of Alternative Brand	14
Other	16
	200

There are 8 reasons (categories). If the reasons were uniformly distributed, the expected frequency for each reason would be 200/8 = 25. The value of chi-square is calculated from this formula:

$$\chi^2 = \sum_{i=1}^{k} \frac{(O_i - E_i)^2}{E_i}$$

where k is the number of categories, O_i is the observed frequency for a given category, and E_i is the expected frequency for the same category. The degrees of freedom for the goodness of fit test are $k - 1$. The CHISQ.TEST tool reports the probability of the obtained value of chi square if the null hypothesis is true. However, this tool does not calculate chi square. The CHISQ.INV function can be used to find values of chi-square given the probability and the degrees of freedom, but as mentioned, it does not work in the extremes of the distribution, so I only use it to find critical values.

The following screenshot (see Figure 9-1) shows the formulas used to calculate the expected frequencies, the value of chi square (cell D10), and the p-level of the obtained chi square using the

`CHISQ.DIST` function (cell D11). The results of the test are shown in the Value View in Figure 9-2. Note in the Formula Bar the use of the `CHISQ.DIST` function to find the p value.

Reason for Switching Brands	Observed	Expected	$(O - E)^2/E$
Preferred Brand Not Available	32	=200/COUNT($C$3:$C$10)	=(C3-D3)^2/D3
Less Expensive Alternative	17	=200/COUNT($C$3:$C$10)	=(C4-D4)^2/D4
New Brand Available	16	=200/COUNT($C$3:$C$10)	=(C5-D5)^2/D5
Dissatisfied with Current Brand	37	=200/COUNT($C$3:$C$10)	=(C6-D6)^2/D6
Just Looking for a Change	33	=200/COUNT($C$3:$C$10)	=(C7-D7)^2/D7
Negative Publicity about Current Brand	35	=200/COUNT($C$3:$C$10)	=(C8-D8)^2/D8
Positive Promotion of Alternative Brand	14	=200/COUNT($C$3:$C$10)	=(C9-D9)^2/D9
Other	16	=200/COUNT($C$3:$C$10)	=(C10-D10)^2/D10
	=SUM(C3:C10)	=SUM(D3:D10)	=SUM(E3:E10)
			=CHISQ.DIST(28.16,7,FALSE

Figure 9-1. Formulas used for chi-square test

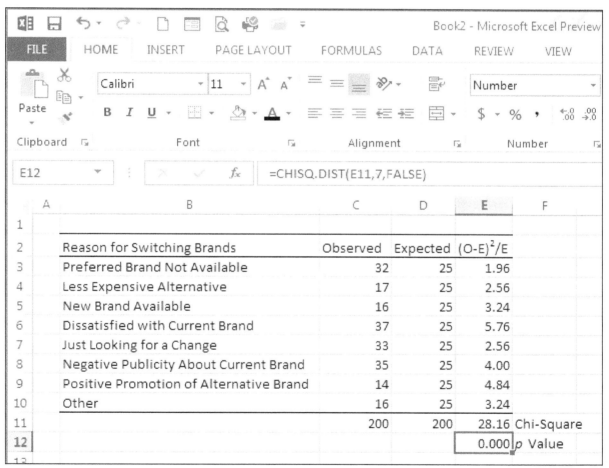

Figure 9-2. Chi-square test results

As an alternative to the calculations we just performed, the `CHISQ.TEST` function will return the p value, which is really not zero, but something less than .001. We can then use the `CHISQ.INV.RT` function to determine the value of chi-square. Here is how to do that. See Figure 9-3 for the formulas and Figure 9-4 for the values.

Reason for Switching Brands	Observed	Expected
Preferred Brand Not Available	32	=200/COUNT($C$3:$C$10)
Less Expensive Alternative	17	=200/COUNT($C$3:$C$10)
New Brand Available	16	=200/COUNT($C$3:$C$10)
Dissatisfied with Current Brand	37	=200/COUNT($C$3:$C$10)
Just Looking for a Change	33	=200/COUNT($C$3:$C$10)
Negative Publicity about Current Brand	35	=200/COUNT($C$3:$C$10)
Positive Promotion of Alternative Brand	14	=200/COUNT($C$3:$C$10)
Other	16	=200/COUNT($C$3:$C$10)

Using CHISQ.TEST to determine p value	=CHISQ.TEST(C3:C10,D3:D10)
Using CHISQ.INV to determine chi-square	=CHISQ.INV.RT(C12,7)

Figure 9-3. Using CHISQ.TEST and CHISQ.INV.RT functions to calculate p and chi-square

	A	B	C	D	E
1					
2		Reason for Switching Brands	Observed	Expected	
3		Preferred Brand Not Available	32	25	
4		Less Expensive Alternative	17	25	
5		New Brand Available	16	25	
6		Dissatisfied with Current Brand	37	25	
7		Just Looking for a Change	33	25	
8		Negative Publicity about Current Brand	35	25	
9		Positive Promotion of Alternative Brand	14	25	
10		Other	16	25	
11					
12		Using CHISQ.TEST to determine p value	0.000205685		
13		Using CHISQ.INV to determine chi-square	28.16		
14					

Figure 9-4. Using Excel functions avoids further calculations

A Chi-Square Goodness-of-Fit Test Template

Although the calculations shown above are routine, they are laborious. A worksheet template for the chi-square goodness of fit test makes the calculations less time consuming. The user inserts the observed data values, and the template automates the calculations. The current problem is shown in the template (See Figure 9-5). The template is available at the companion web page. To make these templates more generally useful, I avoid using the newer Excel 2010 functions so that people with previous Excel versions can also use the templates.

	A	B	C	D	E	F	G	H	I	J	K
1	Level	Observed	Expected		Results						
2	1	32	25		Count (k)	8					
3	2	17	25		Sum	200					
4	3	16	25		χ^2	28.1600					
5	4	37	25		df (k - 1)	7					
6	5	33	25		p (χ^2)	0.0002					
7	6	35	25								
8	7	14	25								
9	8	16	25								

This worksheet template performs a chi-square test of goodness of fit. The expected values are based on the null hypothesis of no difference in distribution of observations in the different levels of the categorical variable.

Enter up to 100 observed frequencies in the green-shaded data entry area, beginning in cell B2. Each row should represent a level of the categorical variable. The template counts the number of categories, calculates expected frequencies according to the null hypothesis, calculates chi-square, and calculates the probability of the observed value of chi-square if the null hypothesis is true.

The worksheet is protected to keep you from accidentally changing the formulas.

Figure 9-5. Chi-square goodness-of-fit template

Chi-Square Goodness-of-Fit Test with Unequal Expected Frequencies

Let us return to a previous data set and determine whether the body temperature data from Table 5-1 are normally distributed. You can use your knowledge of the standard normal distribution and skills with the FREQUENCY function of Excel to make this test simple. You will have to provide bins for your test. Say you chose 10 bins (an arbitrary but convenient choice). You will then have a chi-square test with 9 degrees of freedom. Because you expect the data to be normally distributed, the categories will have unequal expected values, as discussed above. Use the STANDARDIZE function to convert the temperatures to z scores, the NORMSDIST function to find the expected percentage for each bin, and the FREQUENCY function to find the observed frequencies in each interval. Because you have already learned the FREQUENCY function in Chapter 2, the illustration is not extensive, but it would be good practice to see if you can replicate the findings. See the Formula View in Figure 9-6, the Value View in Table 9-2, and the results of the chi-square test using the template in Figure 9-7. To make use of the template, all you need to do is paste in the observed and expected frequencies from Table 9-2. Remember that the bins are the upper limits of the class intervals being used. In this example, the bins are in cells D2:D11. Note again the helpful use of named ranges to indicate which array is being used.

Bin	z BIN	Observed	Expected_Pct	Expected_Count
96.5	=STANDARDIZE(D2,AVERAGE(temp),STDEV(temp))	=FREQUENCY(temp,D2:D11)	=NORMSDIST(E2)	=G2*130
97	=STANDARDIZE(D3,AVERAGE(temp),STDEV(temp))	=FREQUENCY(temp,D2:D11)	=NORMSDIST(E3)-NORMSDIST(E2)	=G3*130
97.5	=STANDARDIZE(D4,AVERAGE(temp),STDEV(temp))	=FREQUENCY(temp,D2:D11)	=NORMSDIST(E4)-NORMSDIST(E3)	=G4*130
98	=STANDARDIZE(D5,AVERAGE(temp),STDEV(temp))	=FREQUENCY(temp,D2:D11)	=NORMSDIST(E5)-NORMSDIST(E4)	=G5*130
98.5	=STANDARDIZE(D6,AVERAGE(temp),STDEV(temp))	=FREQUENCY(temp,D2:D11)	=NORMSDIST(E6)-NORMSDIST(E5)	=G6*130
99	=STANDARDIZE(D7,AVERAGE(temp),STDEV(temp))	=FREQUENCY(temp,D2:D11)	=NORMSDIST(E7)-NORMSDIST(E6)	=G7*130
99.5	=STANDARDIZE(D8,AVERAGE(temp),STDEV(temp))	=FREQUENCY(temp,D2:D11)	=NORMSDIST(E8)-NORMSDIST(E7)	=G8*130
100	=STANDARDIZE(D9,AVERAGE(temp),STDEV(temp))	=FREQUENCY(temp,D2:D11)	=NORMSDIST(E9)-NORMSDIST(E8)	=G9*130
100.5	=STANDARDIZE(D10,AVERAGE(temp),STDEV(temp))	=FREQUENCY(temp,D2:D11)	=NORMSDIST(E10)-NORMSDIST(E9)	=G10*130
101	=STANDARDIZE(D11,AVERAGE(temp),STDEV(temp))	=FREQUENCY(temp,D2:D11)	=NORMSDIST(E11)-NORMSDIST(E10)	=G11*130

Figure 9-6. Chi-square test for normality of distribution (Formula View)

Table 9-9-1. Value View of previous figure

Bin	z BIN	Observed	Expected_Pct	Expected_Count
96.5	-2.4	2	0.009	1.108
97.0	-1.7	5	0.036	4.639
97.5	-1.0	14	0.109	14.198
98.0	-0.3	30	0.214	27.760
98.5	0.3	30	0.267	34.694
99.0	1.0	35	0.213	27.722
99.5	1.7	11	0.109	14.159
100.0	2.4	2	0.036	4.620
100.5	3.1	0	0.007	0.962
101.0	3.8	1	0.001	0.128

	A	B	C	D	E	F	G	H	I	J	K
1	Level	Observed	Expected		Results						
2	1	2	1.107721236		Count (k)	10					
3	2	5	4.638926756		Sum	130					
4	3	14	14.19756899		χ^2	12.58189424					
5	4	30	27.75989599		df (k - 1)	9					
6	5	30	34.69445279		p (χ^2)	0.182455411					
7	6	35	27.72170909								
8	7	11	14.15851927								
9	8	2	4.619788778								
10	9	0	0.96221339								
11	10	1	0.127792471								
12											
13											
14											
15											
16											
17											
18											
19											
20											

This worksheet template performs a chi-square test of goodness of fit for equal or unequal expected frequencies.

Enter up to 100 observed frequencies in the green-shaded data entry area, beginning in cell B2. In the adjacent cells beginning in cell C2, enter the expected frequency under the null hypohtesis.

Each row should represent a level of the categorical variable. The template counts the number of categories, calculates chi-square, and calculates the probability of the observed value of chi-square if the null hypothesis is true.

The worksheet is protected to keep you from accidentally changing the formulas.

Figure 9-7. Chi-square template for unequal expected frequencies

Notice several things about Figure 9-7. This template can be used with equal expected frequencies, too, though it involves a little more work than the template for equal frequencies, as the expected frequencies have to be supplied here. Excel stored the numbers as precisely as it could. The observed counts clearly must be whole numbers because they are discrete, but expected counts can be fractional. Finally, observe that the non-significant value of chi square indicates that the data do not depart significantly from the expected normal distribution. This is the standard interpretation of goodness-of-fit tests. Failure to reject the null hypothesis indicates that the data may be considered to be described by or to "fit" the proposed distribution. Statistical significance, on the other hand, means that the data depart from the proposed distribution.

Chi-Square Test of Independence

The following formula is used to calculate the value of chi-square for a test of independence:

$$\chi^2 = \sum_{i=1}^{R} \sum_{j=1}^{C} \frac{(O_{ij} - E_{ij})^2}{E_{ij}}$$

where R is the number of rows (representing one categorical variable) and C is the number of columns (representing the second categorical variable). The double summation simply means to add up $(O - E)^2/E$ for every cell in the table.

The expected frequencies under the null hypothesis are based on a presumed lack of association between the row and column variables. To calculate expected frequencies for the chi-square test of independence, the row and column marginal subtotals are multiplied for a given cell, and the product is divided by the total number of observations. This process is greatly simplified by the use of formulas in Excel. The degrees of freedom for the test of independence are $(R - 1) \times (C - 1)$. Once the expected frequencies are calculated, the CHITEST tool can return the p level for the chi-square the test of independence, though not the value of chi-square.

The following hypothetical data represent the frequency of use of various computational tools by statistics professors in departments of psychology, business, and mathematics (see Table 9-3).

Table 9-9-2. Computational tools used in statistics classes

Department	SPSS	Excel	Minitab	Total
Psychology	21	6	4	31
Business	6	19	8	33
Mathematics	5	7	12	24
Total	32	32	24	88

The worksheet template shown in Figure 9-8 was used to calculate the value of chi-square and test its significance. The results of the test also appear in Figure 9-8. Because these calculations are repetitive, it is beneficial to create and save a generic worksheet template for the chi-square test of independence and then to replace the observed values with new values for new tests. The chi-square template is freely available for personal and educational use and can be obtained from the companion web site.

The significant value of chi square indicates that the choice of a computational tool is associated with the department in which the statistics course is taught, $\chi^2 (4, N = 88) = 26.88$, $p < .001$. The template also calculates Cramér's V (or the φ coefficient for 1 df) as a measure of effect size for the chi-square test of independence (Gravetter & Wallnau, 2008). Rea and Parker (1992) provide a guide to interpreting the magnitude of the effect size for chi-square tests of independence (see Table 9-4). In the current case, the effect size index would indicate a moderate association between the department and the computational tool of choice.

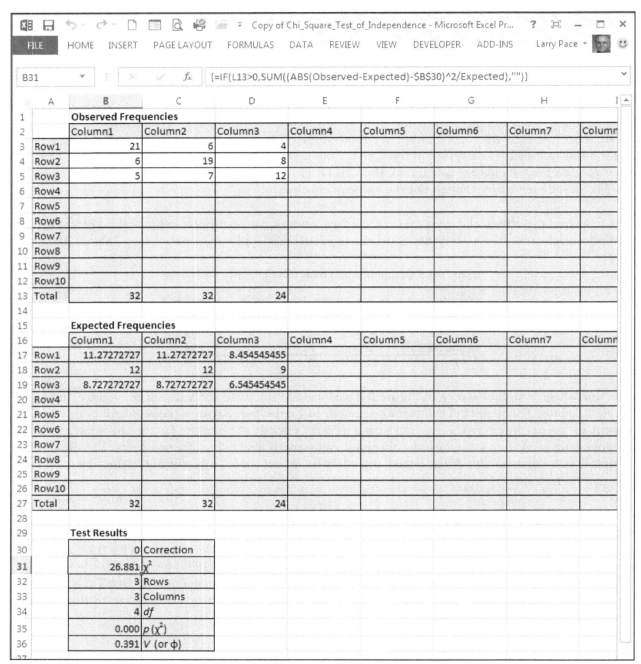

Figure 9-8. Worksheet template for chi-square test of independence

Table 9-9-3. Guide to interpreting effect size for φ or Cramér's *V*

Value of φ or Cramér's *V*	Strength of Association
.00 and under .10	Negligible association
.10 and under .20	Weak association
.20 and under .40	Moderate association
.40 and under .60	Relatively strong association
.60 and under .80	Strong association
.80 to 1.00	Very strong association

In the worksheet template (see Figure 9-8), Yates' correction for continuity is applied if the data are a 2 × 2 contingency table (1 degree of freedom). This correction is required because the binomial distribution is discrete while the normal distribution is continuous (Hays, 1973). The reader should note that the chi-square test for a two-way contingency table, even with the Yates correction, is an approximate test. When expected frequencies are low, the Fisher exact test is a very useful alternative to chi-square for examining a 2 × 2 table of independent observations. The Fisher test gives the one-tailed probability that the particular level of association or one even stronger would be observed if the null hypothesis of no relationship was true (Rosenthal & Rosnow, 2008).

THE BOTTOM LINE
- Chi-square tests compare expected frequencies under a null hypothesis with observed frequencies.
- Chi-square tests are suitable for categorical or qualitative data.
- One-way chi-square tests (multiple categories of a single qualitative variable) are called goodness-of-fit tests.
- Two-way chi-square tests (two or more categories of two qualitative variables) are called tests of independence.
- Excel provides the CHIDIST, CHIINV, and CHITEST functions. There is no chi-square test in the Analysis ToolPak.
- The CHIINV function does not work in the extremes of the chi-square distribution.
- Chi-square test templates for goodness-of-fit tests for both equal and unequal frequencies and for tests of independence are available at the companion web page.

Chapter 9 Exercises

1. DuPont conducts an annual survey of automobile paint color preferences, and the following distribution was found in 2011 (source: DuPont Automotive Systems 2011 Global Color Popularity Report):

White	22%
Silver	22%
Black	20%
Gray	13%
Red	7%
Blue	6%
Brown/Beige	5%
Other	5%

Assume you took a random sample of 100 automobiles at the local Walmart parking lot and found the following distribution. At an alpha level of .05, are the colors distributed according to expectation? Use a chi-square test of goodness of fit with unequal expected frequencies.

Color	Number
White	23
Silver	20
Black	23
Gray	10
Red	9
Blue	5
Brown/Beige	6
Other	4
Total	100

2. The following data show the number of recorded amateur and professional boxing-related fatalities by weight class since 1920. Conduct a chi-square test of goodness of fit to determine if the boxing-related fatalities are equally distributed across weight classifications (source: http://ejmas.com/jcs/jcsart_svinth_a_0700.htm).

Classification	Fatalities
Flyweight	54
Bantamweight	67
Featherweight	102
Lightweight	127
Welterweight	116
Middleweight	93
Light heavyweight	50
Heavyweight	53

3. Assume that the data in Table 9-3 were expanded to include the following additional information:

Department	SPSS	Excel	Minitab	SAS	Matlab	Fathom	Total
Psychology	21	6	4	4	4	8	47
Business	6	19	8	10	5	4	52
Mathematics	5	7	12	4	11	3	42
Education	3	4	5	4	5	12	33
Total	35	36	29	22	25	27	174

Conduct a chi-square test of independence. Calculate and interpret Cramér's V as a measure of effect size.

4. The following data represent the number of gold, silver, and bronze medals for the top 10 countries in the Summer 2012 Olympics. Conduct a goodness-of-fit test to determine if the total number of medals is equally distributed by country.

Nation	Gold	Silver	Bronze	Total
United States	46	29	29	104
China	38	27	23	88
Russia	24	26	32	82
Great Britain	29	17	19	65
Germany	11	19	14	44
Japan	7	14	17	38
Australia	7	16	12	35
France	11	11	12	34
South Korea	13	8	7	28
Italy	8	9	11	28

5. Using the data from the previous exercise, conduct a chi-square test of independence to determine if the distributions of gold, silver, and bronze medals are independent of the country.

Appendix A—Statistical Functions in Excel

Statistical Term	Definitional Formula	Excel 2010 Function	Legacy Excel Function
Summation	$\sum_{i=1}^{n} x_i$	SUM(X)	SUM(X)
Mean, Expected Value	$\overline{x} = \dfrac{\sum_{i=1}^{n} x_i}{n}$	AVERAGE(X)	AVERAGE(X)
Sum of Squares	$SS = \sum_{i=1}^{n} \left(x_i - \overline{x}\right)^2$	DEVSQ(X)	DEVSQ(X)
Population Variance	$\sigma_x^2 = \dfrac{\sum_{i=1}^{N} (x_i - \mu)^2}{N}$	VAR.P(X)	VARP(X)
Population Standard Deviation	$\sigma_x = \sqrt{\sigma_x^2}$	STDEV.P(X)	STDEVP(X)
Sample Variance	$s_x^2 = \dfrac{\sum_{i=1}^{n} (x_i - \overline{x})^2}{n-1}$	VAR.S(X)	VAR(X)
Sample Standard Deviation	$s_x = \sqrt{s_x^2}$	STDEV.S(X)	STDEV(X)
Population Covariance	$\sigma_{xy} = \dfrac{\sum_{i=1}^{N} (x_i - \mu_x)(y_i - \mu_y)}{N}$	COVARIANCE.P(X, Y)	COVAR(X, Y)
Sample Covariance	$s_{xy} = \dfrac{\sum_{i=1}^{n} (x_i - \overline{x})(y_i - \overline{y})}{n-1}$	COVARIANCE.S(X, Y)	COVAR(X, Y)*(n/(n-1))
Correlation Coefficient	$r_{xy} = \dfrac{s_{xy}}{s_x s_y}$	CORREL(X, Y)	CORREL(X, Y)

Replace X or Y in the Excel function with the reference to the applicable data range, e.g., A1:A25, or the name of the range. Replace n with the number of observations (in the covariance calculation, replace n with the number of *pairs* of observations).

Appendix B—Answers to Odd-Numbered Exercises

Chapter 1 Exercises

1. Not answered.

3. The answers appear below:

   a. What is 999 divided by 222? **4.5**
   b. What is 621 + 2443 + 12232 + 1232? **16528**
   c. Find the square root of 325351. **570.395**
   d. What is 33 to the fourth power? **1185921**
   e. Calculate the sum of the scores for Test1 in your example spreadsheet (see Figure 1-14). **342**
   f. Calculate the average score for Test1 in the example spreadsheet. **68.4**
   g. What is the average test score for Kim in the example spreadsheet? **61.0**

Chapter 2 Exercises

1. The results appear below. The requested statistics are highlighted.

Scores	
Mean	73.22857143
Standard Error	1.282779096
Median	73
Mode	67
Standard Deviation	7.589023475
Sample Variance	57.59327731
Kurtosis	0.669474779
Skewness	-0.410462284
Range	35
Minimum	52
Maximum	87
Sum	2563
Count	35
Confidence Level(95.0%)	2.60692076

3. The statistics appear below. There appears to be a small increase in wages from 2001 to 2002

179

	PctChg
Mean	2.314771013
Standard Error	0.154656928
Median	2.556827893
Mode	#N/A
Standard Deviation	1.104471384
Sample Variance	1.219857038
Kurtosis	0.992320335
Skewness	-0.974282328
Range	5.391060467
Minimum	-0.853896034
Maximum	4.537164432
Sum	118.0533217
Count	51
Confidence Level(95.0%)	0.310637576

Chapter 3 Exercises

1. The results appear below:

Region	Average 2002 Wages
Midwest	$32,544.25
Northeast	$38,987.44
South	$34,001.18
West	$33,256.85

3. The results appear below:

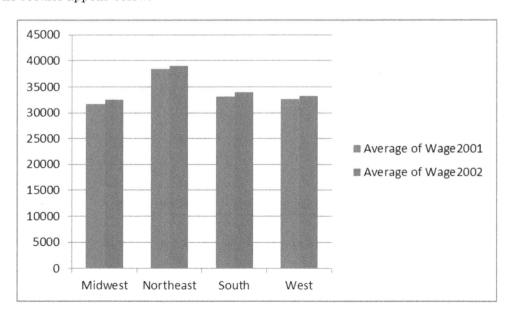

5. Results appear below:

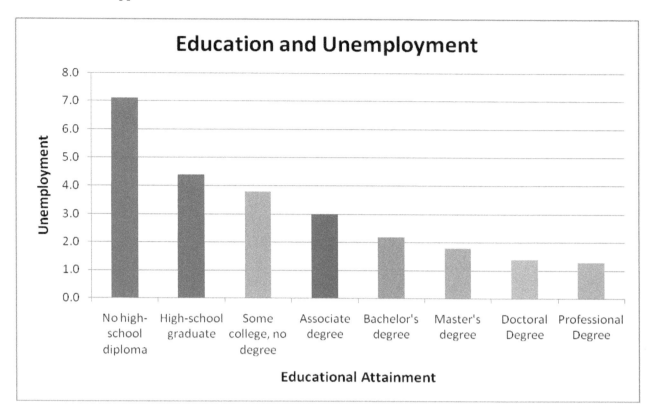

7. It appears that here is a stronger relationship between age and salary for males than for females:

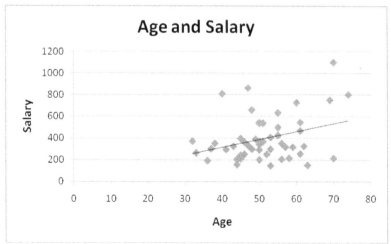

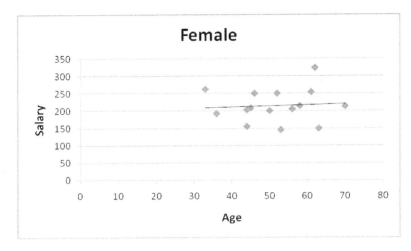

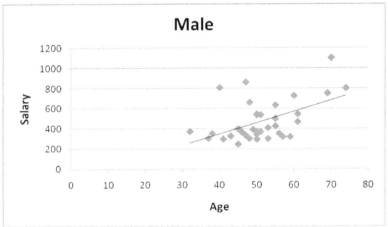

Chapter 4 Exercises

1. A normal distribution has a mean of 75 with a standard deviation of 10.
   a. About what percent of observations are greater than 95? **$z = 2.0$, approximately 2.3% are greater.**
   b. About what percent of observations are lower than 65? **$z = -1.0$, approximately 15.9% are lower.**
   c. About what percent of observations are between 60 and 90? **$z_2 = 1.5$, $z_1 = -1.5$, approximately 86.6% are between 60 and 90.**

3. Assume that the commute time from downtown Chicago to O'Hare Airport using the Chicago Transit Authority train system is normally distributed with a mean of 65 minutes and a standard deviation of 5 minutes.
   a. What is the z score associated with a commute time of 53 minutes? **$z = -2.4$**
   b. About what percent of commutes take less than 60 minutes? **$z = -1.0$, approximately 15.9% take less than 60 minutes.**
   c. About what percent of commutes will be longer than 70 minutes? **$z = 1.0$, approximately 15.9% are longer than 70 minutes.**
   d. About what percent of commutes will be between 60 and 70 minutes? **$z_2 = 1$, $z_1 = -1$, approximately 68.3% are between 60 and 70 minutes.**

Chapter 5 Exercises

1. Results are below. You can reject the null hypothesis and conclude that the average change was greater than zero. The value of Cohen's d suggests a large effect size.

Sample Size	51
Population Mean μ_0	0
Sample Mean	2.314771013
Standard Deviation	1.104471384
Standard Error	0.154656928
t	14.96713429
df	50
Two-tailed Probability	0.000
Left-tailed Probability	1.000
Right-tailed Probability	0.000
Cohen's d	2.10
Mean Difference	2.314771013
95% Confidence Interval	

Lower Limit	Upper Limit
2.004133431	2.625408596

3. Results of the test using the worksheet template are below. You can reject the null hypothesis and conclude that the body temperatures of females are higher than those of males. The value of Cohen's d suggests a small effect size.

Statistic	Group1	Group2
Sum	6376.8	6395.6
Count	65	65
Mean	98.10461538	98.39384615
Variance	0.488259615	0.552774038
Standard Deviation	0.698755762	0.743487753
Pooled Variance	0.520516827	
Pooled Standard Deviation	0.721468521	
Mean Difference	-0.289230769	
Standard Error of Mean Difference	0.12655395	
df	128	
t obtained	-2.285434538	
one-tailed probability	0.0120	
two-tailed probability	0.0239	
Cohen's d	0.400891738	

95% Confidence Interval	Lower Limit	Upper Limit
Mean Difference: -0.289230769230755	-0.539639378	-0.03882216

Chapter 6 Exercises

1. Results appear below. Because the overall F ratio is not significant, post hoc comparisons are unwarranted.

ANOVA

Source of Variation	SS	df	MS	F	P-value	F crit
Between Groups	271363844.840	3	90454614.947	2.515	0.070	2.802
Within Groups	1690354238.846	47	35964983.805			
Total	1961718083.686	50				

3. Results are below. If prices are equal, the fleet manager should purchase Brand B.

ANOVA

Source of Variation	SS	df	MS	F	P-value	F crit
Between Groups	17.049	2	8.525	12.742	0.001	3.885
Within Groups	8.028	12	0.669			
Total	25.077	14				

Table of Mean Differences

	Brand A	Brand B	Brand C
Brand A	-	1.64*	-0.94
Brand B	-	-	-2.58*
Brand C	-	-	-

HSD   1.379
*p < .05

Chapter 7 Exercises

1. Results are below. The training program was effective and is still effective six months later.

ANOVA

Source of Variation	SS	df	MS	F	P-value	F crit
Rows	203.6	9	22.622	26.789	0.000	2.250
Columns	110.7	3	36.900	43.697	0.000	2.960
Error	22.8	27	0.844			
Total	337.1	39				

Table of Mean Differences

	Before	After	3Mo	6Mo
Before	-	1.6*	3.6*	4.2*
After	-	-	2*	2.6*
3Mo	-	-	-	0.6
6Mo	-	-	-	-

HSD   1.126

*p < .05

3. Results are below. The judges' ratings are not consistent. However, the only significant comparison is between Judge 2 and Judge1. The difference between Judge 4 and Judge 2 approaches significance.

ANOVA

Source of Variation	SS	df	MS	F	P-value	F crit
Rows	122.5	5	24.500	19.865	0.000	2.901
Columns	17.5	3	5.833	4.730	0.016	3.287
Error	18.5	15	1.233			
Total	158.5	23				

Table of Mean Differences

	Judge 1	Judge 2	Judge 3	Judge 4
Judge 1	-	2.000*	1.500	0.167
Judge 2	-	-	-0.500	-1.833
Judge 3	-	-	-	-1.333
Judge 4	-	-	-	-

HSD   1.8496

*p < .05

Chapter 8 Exercises

1. Results using the correlation and regression worksheet template are shown below. We can conclude that there is a significant negative relationship between weekly wage and unemployment rate. People who make higher wages are less likely to be unemployed.

Results	X	Y
Mean	941.375	3.125
Standard Deviation	393.033	1.957
Variance	154475.125	3.831
Pairs	8	

Correlation	-0.89
r^2	0.80
t	-4.83
df	6
$p(t)$	0.003
Regression Coefficient	-0.004
Intercept	7.307

3. Results are below:

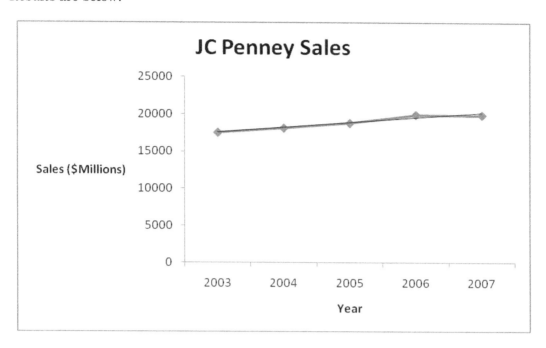

SUMMARY OUTPUT

Regression Statistics	
Multiple R	0.970
R Square	0.942
Adjusted R Square	0.922
Standard Error	295.281
Observations	5

ANOVA

	df	SS	MS	F	Significance F
Regression	1	4226300.100	4226300.100	48.472	0.006
Residual	3	261573.100	87191.033		
Total	4	4487873.200			

	Coefficients	Standard Error	t Stat	P-value	Lower 95%	Upper 95%
Intercept	16880.3	309.694	54.506	0.000	15894.717	17865.883
Index	650.1	93.376	6.962	0.006	352.935	947.265

Year	Forecast
2008	20780.9
2009	21431.0
2010	22081.1

Chapter 9 Exercises

1. The expected and observed frequencies are below:

Level	Observed	Expected
1	23	22
2	20	22
3	23	20
4	10	13
5	9	7
6	5	6
7	6	5
8	4	5

The chi-square test is not significant. We can assume the observed frequencies do not differ significantly from expectation.

Results	
Count (k)	8
Sum	100
χ^2	2.507675658
df (k - 1)	7
p (χ^2)	0.926517972

3. The results of the chi-square test of independence using the worksheet template are shown below. Reject the null hypothesis and conclude that there is an association between the department and the kind of software used:

Test Results

0	Correction
56.237	χ^2
4	Rows
6	Columns
15	df
0.000	p (χ^2)
0.328	V (or ϕ)

5. The chi-square test of independence shows that the distribution of medals is independent of country.

Test Results

0	Correction
25.636	χ^2
10	Rows
3	Columns
18	df
0.108	p (χ^2)
0.153	V (or ϕ)

Appendix C—Critical Values of q (the Studentized Range Statistic)

df_w	α	Number of Means								
		2	3	4	5	6	7	8	9	10
5	0.05	3.64	4.60	5.22	5.67	6.03	6.33	6.58	6.80	6.99
	0.01	5.70	6.98	7.80	8.42	8.91	9.32	9.67	9.97	10.24
6	0.05	3.46	4.34	4.90	5.30	5.63	5.90	6.12	6.32	6.49
	0.01	5.24	6.33	7.03	7.56	7.97	8.32	8.61	8.87	9.10
7	0.05	3.34	4.16	4.68	5.06	5.36	5.61	5.82	6.00	6.16
	0.01	4.95	5.92	6.54	7.01	7.37	7.68	7.94	8.17	8.37
8	0.05	3.26	4.04	4.53	4.89	5.17	5.40	5.60	5.77	5.92
	0.01	4.75	5.64	6.20	6.62	6.96	7.24	7.47	7.37	7.86
9	0.05	3.20	3.95	4.41	4.76	5.02	5.24	5.43	5.59	5.74
	0.01	4.60	5.43	5.96	6.35	6.66	6.91	7.13	7.33	7.49
10	0.05	3.15	3.88	4.33	4.65	4.91	5.12	5.30	5.46	5.60
	0.01	4.48	5.27	5.77	6.14	6.43	6.67	6.87	7.05	7.21
11	0.05	3.11	3.82	4.26	4.57	4.82	5.03	5.20	5.35	5.49
	0.01	4.39	5.15	5.62	5.97	6.25	6.48	6.67	6.84	6.99
12	0.05	3.08	3.77	4.20	4.51	4.75	4.95	5.12	5.27	5.39
	0.01	4.32	5.05	5.50	5.84	6.10	6.32	6.51	6.67	6.81
13	0.05	3.06	3.73	4.15	4.45	4.69	4.88	5.05	5.19	5.32
	0.01	4.25	4.96	5.40	5.73	5.98	6.19	6.37	6.53	6.67
14	0.05	3.03	3.70	4.11	4.41	4.64	4.83	4.99	5.13	5.25
	0.01	4.21	4.89	5.32	5.63	5.88	6.08	6.26	6.41	6.54
15	0.05	3.01	3.67	4.08	4.37	4.59	4.78	4.94	5.08	5.20
	0.01	4.17	4.84	5.25	5.56	5.80	5.99	6.16	6.31	6.44
16	0.05	3.00	3.65	4.05	4.33	4.56	4.74	4.90	5.03	5.15
	0.01	4.13	4.79	5.19	5.49	5.72	5.92	6.08	6.22	6.35
17	0.05	2.98	3.63	4.02	4.30	4.52	4.70	4.86	4.99	5.11
	0.01	4.10	4.74	5.14	5.43	5.66	5.85	6.01	6.15	6.27
18	0.05	2.97	3.61	4.00	4.28	4.49	4.67	4.82	4.96	5.07
	0.01	4.07	4.70	5.09	5.38	5.60	5.79	5.94	6.08	6.20
19	0.05	2.96	3.59	3.98	4.25	4.47	4.65	4.79	4.92	5.04
	0.01	4.05	4.67	5.05	5.33	5.55	5.73	5.89	6.02	6.14
20	0.05	2.95	3.58	3.96	4.23	4.45	4.62	4.77	4.90	5.01
	0.01	4.02	4.64	5.02	5.29	5.51	5.69	5.84	5.97	6.09
24	0.05	2.92	3.53	3.90	4.17	4.37	4.54	4.68	4.81	4.92
	0.01	3.96	4.55	4.91	5.17	5.37	5.54	5.69	5.81	5.92
30	0.05	2.89	3.49	3.85	4.10	4.30	4.46	4.60	4.72	4.82
	0.01	3.89	4.45	4.80	5.05	5.24	5.40	5.54	5.65	5.76
40	0.05	2.86	3.44	3.79	4.04	4.23	4.39	4.52	4.63	4.73
	0.01	3.82	4.37	4.70	4.93	5.11	5.26	5.39	5.50	5.60
60	0.05	2.83	3.40	3.74	3.98	4.16	4.31	4.44	4.55	4.65
	0.01	3.76	4.28	4.59	4.82	4.99	5.13	5.25	5.36	5.45
120	0.05	2.80	3.36	3.68	3.92	4.10	4.24	4.36	4.47	4.56
	0.01	3.70	4.20	4.50	4.71	4.87	5.01	5.12	5.21	5.30
∞	0.05	2.77	3.31	3.63	3.86	4.03	4.17	4.29	4.39	4.47
	0.01	3.64	4.12	4.40	4.60	4.76	4.88	4.99	5.08	5.16

Source: Generated by use of the qtukey() function in the statistical language R.

Appendix D—Getting and Using MegaStat

MegaStat, mentioned in the preface and illustrated briefly in this book, makes Excel a very capable statistics package. MegaStat is an add-in for Excel, and works with versions Excel 2003, 2007, 2010, and 2018. It is also available for Excel Mac 2011, but not for previous versions of Excel for Mac. In this brief appendix, you learn how to get MegaStat and how MegaStat works. Note that like the Analysis ToolPak and other add-ins, MegaStat takes a "snapshot" of the data, and produces static output rather than dynamic output. If you change the data, you must run the analysis again to get updated results.

MegaStat makes up for most of Excel's statistical shortcomings, providing the missing graphics discussed earlier, additional hypothesis tests (including nonparametric tests), and other features found in typical statistics packages. As mentioned in the preface, MegaStat was developed by Professor J. B. Orris of Butler University and is distributed by McGraw-Hill. The add-in is available for a very low price. Here is the link:

http://highered.mcgraw-
hill.com/sites/0077425995/information_center_view0/megastat_.html

To install MegaStat, you must download the add-in and then use the Excel options. Locate the downloaded file and install MegaStat the same way you did the Analysis ToolPak (see Figure D-1):

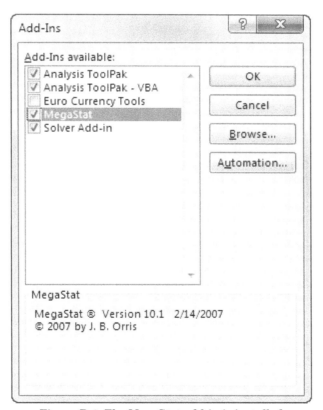

Figure D-1. The MegaStat add-in is installed

With MegaStat installed properly, you will now have a MegaStat option in the Add-Ins group (see Figure D-2).

Figure D-2. The MegaStat add-in is now available

Examine the many options available under the Descriptive Statistics menu in MegaStat (see Figure D-3). We will use the data from Table 5-1 (page 103), which as you recall, are the body temperatures of 130 adults.

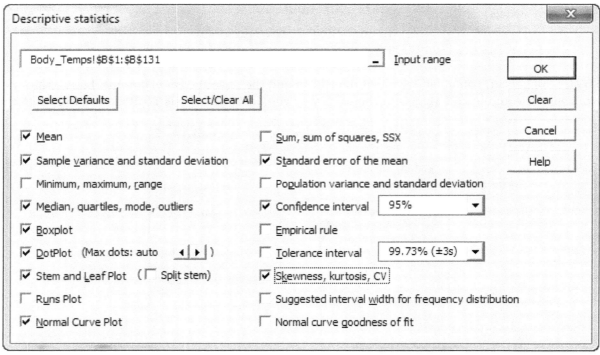

Figure D-3. Descriptive statistics available in MegaStat

Here are the results (partial listing) of the Descriptive statistics tool in MegaStat (Figure D-4). MegaStat adds a worksheet labeled "Output," and all subsequent results are appended to that sheet.

Descriptive statistics	
	Temp
count	130
mean	98.249
sample variance	0.538
sample standard deviation	0.733
standard error of the mean	0.064
confidence interval 95.% lower	98.122
confidence interval 95.% upper	98.376
half-width	0.127
skewness	-0.004
kurtosis	0.780
coefficient of variation (CV)	0.75%
1st quartile	97.800
median	98.300
3rd quartile	98.700
interquartile range	0.900
mode	98.000
low extremes	0
low outliers	2
high outliers	1
high extremes	0

Figure D-4. Descriptive statistics output in MegaStat

Now, let us redo the one-sample t test from Chapter 5. Remember we tested the sample mean against the hypothesized population value of 98.6 degrees Fahrenheit. To perform this test in MegaStat, use the following procedure. Select **Add-Ins > MegaStat > Hypothesis Tests > Mean vs. Hypothesized Value** (see Figure D-5).

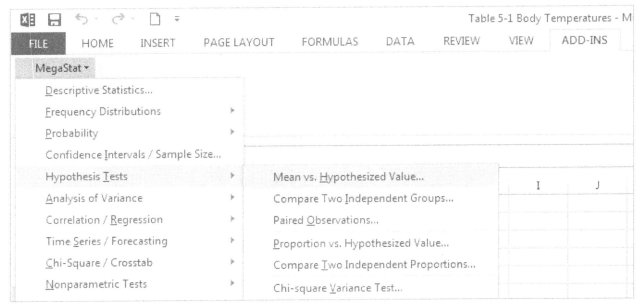

Figure D-5. Select Add-ins > MegaStat > Hypothesis Tests > Mean vs. Hypothesized Value

In the resulting dialog box, note that you can use either summary data or raw data, and that you can perform a *t* test or a *z* test. Fill out the dialog as follows (see Figure D-6):

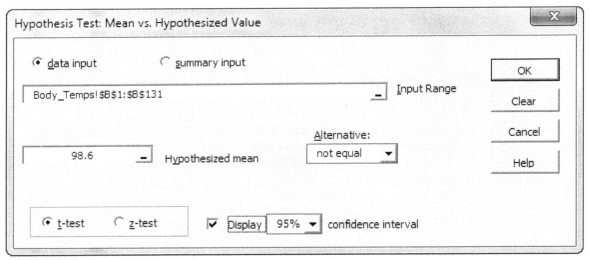

FigureD-6. Completed dialog box for one-sample *t* test

MegaStat performs the test and puts the results in the Output sheet (see Figure D-7).

	A	B	C	D	E	F
1						
2	Hypothesis Test: Mean vs. Hypothesized Value					
3						
4		98.6000	hypothesized value			
5		98.2492	mean Temp			
6		0.7332	std. dev.			
7		0.0643	std. error			
8		130	n			
9		129	df			
10						
11		-5.45	t			
12		2.41E-07	p-value (two-tailed)			
13						
14		98.1220	confidence interval 95.% lower			
15		98.3765	confidence interval 95.% upper			
16		0.1272	margin of error			
17						

Figure D-7. MegaStat Output for the one-sample t test

MegaStat produces the same results as our Excel template, R, and SPSS. Though reassuring, this should also be unsurprising, because all these technologies use the same formulas. You can find online manuals, tutorials, videos, and other resources for MegaStat through a quick web search. I certainly recommend it above all the other available statistics add-ins for Excel. Many of McGraw-Hill's statistics texts include MegaStat as part of the price of the book. You now know enough about MegaStat to understand how to get it, how it works, and how to use it.

Appendix E—Choosing a Statistical Test

Many students struggle with choosing the correct statistical test. Here is a flow chart that may be helpful (see Figure E-1). The chapters in which the tests are explained and illustrated are also listed.

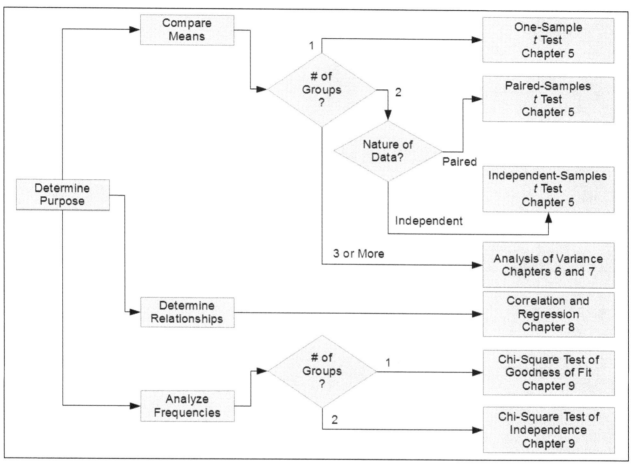

Figure E-1. Choosing a statistical test

References

American Psychological Association. (2010). *Publication manual of the American Psychological Association* (6th ed.). Washington, DC: Author.

Aczel, A., & Sounderpandian, J. (2009). *Complete business statistics* (7th ed.). New York, NY: McGraw-Hill.

Bennett, J., Briggs, W., & Triola, M. (2009). *Statistical reasoning for everyday life* (3rd ed.). New York, NY: Pearson Addison-Wesley.

Cohen, J. (1988). *Statistical power analysis for the behavioral sciences* (2nd ed.). Hillsdale, NJ: Lawrence Erlbaum Associates.

Gravetter, F., & Wallnau, L. (2008). *Essentials of statistics for the behavioral sciences* (6th ed.). Belmont, CA: Thomson Wadsworth.

Grover, C., MacDonald, M., & Vander Veer, E. A. (2007). *Office 2007: The missing manual*. Sebastopol, CA: O'Reilly.

Hays, W. (1973). *Statistics for the social sciences* (2nd ed.). New York, NY: Holt, Rinehart and Winston.

Howell, D. (2008). *Fundamental statistics for the behavioral sciences* (6th ed.). Belmont, CA: Thomson Wadsworth.

Lind, D., Marchal, W. & Wathen, S. (2008). *Basic statistics for business & economics* (6th ed.). New York, NY: McGraw-Hill.

Moore, D., McCabe, G., Duckworth, W., & Sclove, S. (2003). *The practice of business statistics: Using data for decisions*. New York, NY: Freeman.

Pace, L. (2006). *The Excel statistics cookbook* (2nd ed.). Anderson, SC: TwoPaces LLC.

Pace, L. (2006). *Introductory statistics: A cognitive learning approach*. Anderson, SC: TwoPaces LLC.

Pace, L. (2008). *The Excel 2007 data and statistics cookbook* (2nd ed.). Anderson, SC: TwoPaces.com.

Pace, L. (2010a). *Statistical analysis using Excel 2007*. Upper Saddle River, NJ: Pearson Prentice Hall.

Pace, L. (2010b, January). *Templates as transparent teaching tools*. Poster presented at the 2010 conference of the National Institute on the Teaching of Psychology, St. Pete Beach, FL.

Pace, L. (2012a). *Beginning R: An introduction to statistical programming*. New York, NY: Apress.

Pace, L. (2012b). *Point-and-Click! A guide to SPSS for Windows* (5th ed.). Anderson, SC: TwoPaces.com.

Pace, L. (2012c). *Using Microsoft Word to Write Research Papers in APA Style*. Anderson, SC: TwoPaces.com.

Rea, L. & Parker, R. (1992). *Designing and conducting survey research*. San Francisco, CA: Jossey-Boss.

Roscoe, J. (1975). *Fundamental research statistics for the behavioral sciences* (2nd ed.). New York: Holt, Rinehart and Winston.

Rosenthal, R., & Rosnow, R. (2008). *Essentials of behavioral research: methods and data analysis* (3rd ed.). New York: McGraw-Hill.

Studenmund, A. (2006). *Using econometrics: a practical guide* (5th ed.). New York: Pearson Addison-Wesley.

Thorne, M., & Giesen, J. M. (2003). *Statistics for the behavioral sciences* (4th ed.). New York, NY: McGraw-Hill.

Tukey, J. (1949). Comparing individual means in the analysis of variance. *Biometrics, 5*, 99-114.

Tukey, J. (1977). *Exploratory data analysis*. Reading, MA: Addison-Wesley.

Welkowitz, J., Cohen, B., & Ewen, R. (2006). *Introductory statistics for the behavioral sciences* (6th ed.). Hoboken, NJ: John Wiley & Sons.

Index

A

B

C

K

L

M

N

P

R

W

Z